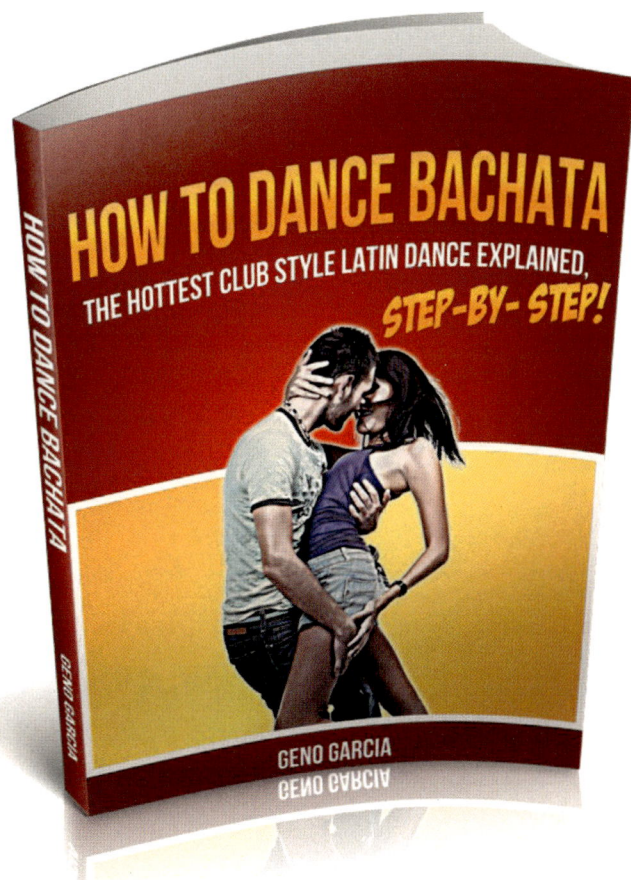

Geno Garcia 2013

All rights reserved. No part of this book may be reproduced or transmitted in any form or by any means, electronic or mechanical, including photocopying, without written permission from the Author of this Book, Geno Garcia.

www.PhoenixSalsaLessons.Com

Table of Contents

Introduction to Bachata Dance & Music..4
The Bachata dance Frame 6
Closed Dance Frame with Style..10
Bachata 2 Handed, Dance hold..12
Bachata 2 Handed Hold Extra Tips..13
Palm to Palm Bachata Hold..14
How To....Not Step On Your Partners Feet..14
Move # 1 The Bachata Basic, Two Hand Hold...17
Move # 2 Bachata Basic (Closed Dance Frame)..19
Move # 3 The One Armed - Bachata Basic..21
Move # 4 Forward & Back Basic...23
Move # 5 Cross Step Basic...25
Move # 6 Syncopated Bachata Basic   (Dominican Style)....................................29
Move # 7 Palm To Palm Basic..31
Sexy Hair Comb Loop...34
Mans Neck Loops (Right Arm)..36
Move # 8 Mans Neck Loop & Basic..38
Two Arm Neck Wraps/ Loop, Explained...40
Move # 9   Mans 2 Arm Wrap & Basic..41
2 Neck loop the lady..43
Move # 10 The Man Turn...45
Move # 11 Ladies Outside Turn...47
Move # 12 Ladies Inside Turn & Neck Loop..49
Move # 13   Ladies Inside Turn   w/ Left hand..51
Move # 14   The Cradle...53
Move # 15   Hammer Lock (to Left)...57
Move # 16   Hammer Lock to the Right...61
Move # 17   Mans Hammer Lock & Dip under..65
Move # 18   Mans Waist Turn...69
Move # 19   Behind the Back, Hand Switch..71
Move # 20   Cross Hand Turns (mans Right over Left)...73
Move # 21   Mans Inside Turn-Loop & Waist Wrap..75
Move # 22   Turn Combo & Arm Figure four Wrap..77
Move # 23   Cross Turn & Side by Side Basic..79
Move # 24   Forward & Back Basic with Leg Raise...84
Move # 25   Cradle Walk & Neck Wrap Combo..86
Bachata Hip Raise Demonstrated 91
Ladies Arm Styling to Side 93
Move #26   Around the World Dip   (Beginner Level)..96
Move # 27 Around the World Dip (Lowered)...97
Move # 28 Bachata Sit Dip..99

Introduction to Bachata Dance & Music

Bachata dancing is known as a very sensual, romantic, sexy style dance. It stands out because of the mesmerizing hip movements and passionate ways that the dancers embrace one another on the dance floor.

This type of dance can also include spins & turns for both the man & the lady. Watching Bachata dancers you'll also see slow and sensual dips as well as fast & syncopated steps, that match the accents and changes in the music. As well as various twists and turns the dance is stylized and danced in a way that highlights the sexiness & femininity of a woman and the cool masculinity of a man.

There are different styles and approaches to dancing Bachata. The "Dominican style" Bachata, is where you dance syncopated steps, meaning certain steps are taken on half a beat as opposed to a whole beat, like all the other steps in the non syncopated style. This can be a more advanced style to dance.

The style of Bachata that is danced in a night club or socially can look very different than an "exhibition style" of a Bachata performance that you would see for example, at a Bachata competition or Bachata/Salsa Congress. The exhibition style that you may see at a competition or in videos online may focus more or tricks, lifts, dips, and body rolls and other flashy moves designed to excite the crowds. The night club or social dance style has dramatic style and flair, but it stands out mainly because of the sensual way it can be danced with lots of hip movement and passionate holds, or even with the Dominican style approach added to it.

Other people describe the way they dance Bachata, as "Bachata Moderna" and even other styles such as Tango Bachata. So this dance definitely has options to chose from and gives you different ways to express yourself on the dance floor.

Bachata music is a genre of music that originated in the rural country side of the Dominican republic around the early part of the 20th century. Though it began in the Dominican republic, it then moved on to become popular in America, Europe, and currently its popular and danced in many parts of the world.

If your unfamiliar with the music, Bachata music is written in 4/4 timing. Depending on the song the music can be described slow dance music or more of an faster tempo with certain others. Bachata music groups usually have 5 musical instruments to play bass guitar, bongos, electric guitars, rhythm guitars, and guiras.

The music can be described as romantic and the themes of the songs are about heartbreak and the likes. To hear some of the most popular modern day Bachata musicians you can look up...Prince Royce, Romeo Santos, Extreme, and Aventura just to name a few.

Bachata is one of the most popular Latin dances in the world, it's sexy, sensual, romantic, & exciting. Bachata videos on Youtube have hundreds of millions of views. And have videos of bachata events, dancers, and competitions all over the world uploaded daily. The Latin dance clubs, bars, parties, weddings, and dance gatherings love to play Bachata & its gaining more and more popularity every day.

The Bachata Dance Frame

Before we jump into all the sexy and dazzling dance moves Bachata has to offer lets learn some of the important secrets that are behind being a good social dancer, starting most importantly where it all begins, with the basics of the "dance frame". Having a solid dance frame, as well as connection and proper hold with your dance partner keeps you on balance and feeling comfortable in your partners arms.

Its easy to want to overlook some of these basics and jump right into to more sensual and flashy to Bachata moves, but like anything you have to learn how to crawl before you walk. So take your time and learn the basics of the dance positions and holds.

Here's two photos of the Bachata "Closed Dance Frame".

We have the side view of an **"in close" dance frame** and the rear view of a regular **closed dance frame**.

These dancers to give you an idea of the dance hold we'll be using. This is a common hold used in social dance setting like parties, night clubs and dance halls where people dance Bachata.

Closed dance frame, In close   *Rear view, closed dance frame*

Even though you may be dancing with someone you just met, its not uncommon to be in the closed dance frame right away. In the following section we'll cover the important details of how to get in this dance hold the right way.

Getting into Closed Dance Frame

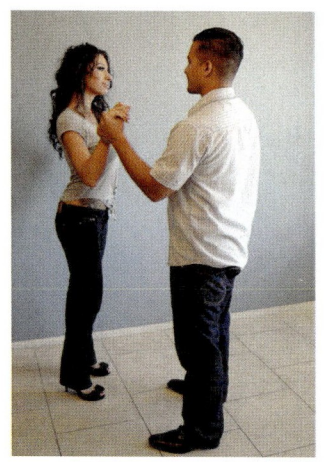

1. Guys take your left hand and reach out and offer it your partner, getting her right hand, with her fingers draped over the space between your index finger and thumb.

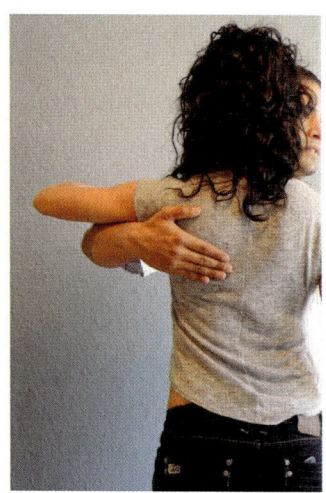

2. Next, once you have your partners hand guide her in, or step into her & reach under her arm and Place your Right hand on your partners shoulder blade, back area. Just place it over her shoulder blade so that your hand is now connected to her back.

3. Prop your arm up under her arm so that you have contact between the two arms, just like in the photo. When your arms connected like this, you make the lady's job as a follower that much easier. You now have a more solid "connection" with your partner. Your movements can be felt easier and she'll feel more secure in your arm. So this form helps you be a better leader on the dance floor.

Bachata Closed Dance Frame, Common Beginner mistakes

Ok first thing that you want to do is **Avoid interlacing your fingers** with your partners, it makes it difficult to get in and out for turns. You'll often seen beginners make this dance frame mistake.

This is something that may feel good & secure to a new dancer, but if you plan to use the turns spins, and other Bachata moves your hands are locked up and can't maneuver as easily freedom they need.

So save this type of hold for when your on a romantic date with you partner that doesn't involve doing Bachata moves.

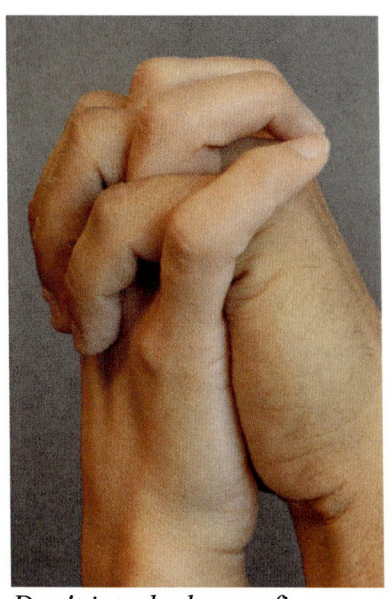

Don't interlock your fingers when you dance Bachata

Too much space between the arms, even though it's fun to put our hand on her hips, it doesn't help much for leading and following. The girls arm is held up just to help demonstrate the lack of contact and connection with the arms.

In the photo above you can see the gap or opening between the man & lady's arm. This type of low hold feels lazy and weak, and doesn't communicate the lead. So look out for and avoid the arm gap.

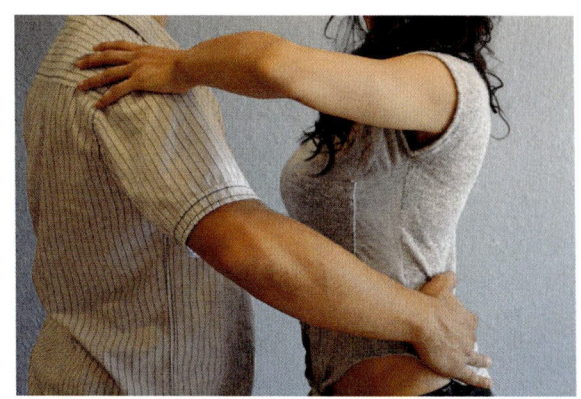

Even though its fun holding her hips, this is an example of what not to do in the dance frame

Dance Frame Common Beginner Mistakes, Continued...

Here's a few other beginner mistakes people have....Either pushing your arms too far forward or pulling them back too much. When your in the closed dance frame you and your partners hands should hang evenly between the two of you. We'll go over these beginner mistakes to avoid so that once you start learning the more flashier and sensual moves you'll have the basics down too.

Leaders here's another thing to look out for in your dance frame. **Pulling your and her arm back** for no good reason. It will be more comfortable for the both of you if your arms are centered evenly between both dancers.

"Arm pulled too far back"

In the photo to the right is an example of having **your arm extended too far forward**, almost to the point of pushing your partner away. Also an uncomfortable position to be in for the lady.

Remember to keep your arms centered between you & her. Not pushed way out behind her or pulling the hands behind you. This almost looks like your keeping her away. But remember Bachata is a dance where its ok to get in close and dance.

"Arm pressing her away"

Closed Dance Frame with Style

In this section we're going to look at other ways to use the Closed dance frame. In the other section on this you'll learned it at the most basic level, which is necessary. Now lets step it up a notch and add some sexiness and style that makes Bachata the hot dance that it is.

First off lets look at the **"Closed dance frame with the hands in close"**. Now guys, for a more intimate feel in the closed dance frame, leaders you can also bring your left hand hand near your heart and keep it positioned there while your in the Bachata closed dance frame. Just like the photo to the right.

closed dance frame "Arms in close"

Aside from being a way to add more of a romantic and intimate feel to the Closed dance frame, this variation comes in handy when your on a crowded dance floor. And you don't have the option of having your arm extended out to the side.

Next is the **Closed dance frame, with your "arm low"** and to your side.

Leaders left arm straightened downward, This second photo shows the arm stretched out downward. This helps add a more in close and seductive feel, to your closed dance frame. Its also useful when the dance floor is too packed with people and you don't have the room to have your normal dance frame hold.

"Closed dance frame, Arms lowered"

Closed Dance frame with style continued....

This is the Closed Dance Frame with the "Arm Stretched out" to the side. This is another type of Bachata dance hold you may see out there. This one is useful to add variety and style to your dancing.

Another thing that you can see in this picture is the lady has her "fingers feathered" on the mans back. This is a softer, more stylized, and more feminine way for the lady to have her left hand in the closed dance

"Closed dance Frame, Arm extended"

Last for the Closed Dance frame is the very **In Close Hold**. This is probably the sexiest of the positions in Bachata. In this hold, you embrace you partner like an in close hug.

The lady's right leg is right in between the mans.
Her right arm around the back of his neck.
The man has his right arm wrapped around her lower back and his left hand to side of the lady's head.
This is a very intimate and sensual dance position, but its also one of the most fun to use, so don't be shy and feel free to use this position because its super common in Bachata.

We just covered lots of information about the closed dance frame, and the closed dance frame with extra sexiness and style. You now have a lot of style options to choose from in the closed frame, ways to dress up the usually plain hold. Don't worry about learning & remembering them all immediately but instead have them in your back pocket as a way to add extra feeling when you dance Bachata. The more you dance the better you'll become about switching it up and varying the moves.

Bachata 2 Handed, Dance hold

Here's a photo of another common Bachata dance hold that you'll be using out on when your dancing.
The 2 handed dance hold. Just like it sounds you hold your partners 2 hands with your 2 hands.

There are some important technique tips that go along with this hold. Most importantly is that the lady's hands go on top of the mans hands.

Having the **lady's hands on top** makes it possible to lead her to the the moves you want her to do. So there's a saying in dance to help you remember this **"lady's on top"**. This means her hands stay on top of the leaders & her arm stays place on top of the leader arm in the frame also.

Two Handed Dance Hold

Guys, you can have your **index finger** on the outside of her hands as an extra lead tool. Having the index finger on the outside of her two hands helps guide her from side to side. But remember less is more with this type of technique so make sure your not pressing your fingers into her hands with way more force than necessary.

Last, the 2 handed hold is a great way to set up turns for the man or the lady. They can be done from the closed dance frame too, but for a newer Bachata dancer I recommend using the 2 hand hold right before turning the lady then you can either stay in this position or get back to a closed dance frame.

Bachata 2 handed hold, opposite side view

Bachata 2 Handed Hold Extra Tips

To the Right is a close up, of the hands in the **"Bachata Two hand hold"**.

Notice the mans **index finger** on the outside of the ladies hands. Ladies hands on top, just like I mentioned before. Plus see how his thumbs aren't squeezing down on the lady's hands. A common beginner mistake guys do is squeezing their thumbs down on the ladies hands.

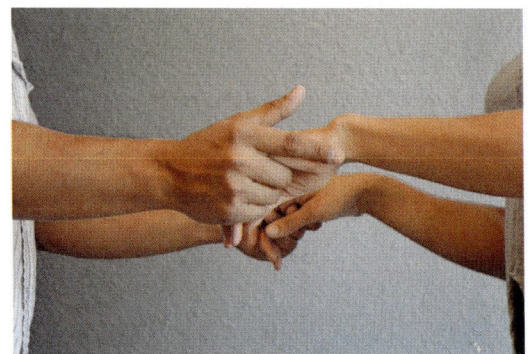

Two hand hold up close w/ correct technique

Don't let your hands float up to your chest area when your in the 2 hand dance hold. Keep your two hands connected to your dance partners and low near your waist area.
As you can see I like to point out a lot of things not to do when your dancing Bachata. Knowing what not to do is also a great way to learn and keeps you from looking silly on the dance floor.

I've noticed when the hands raise up like this, its sometimes the lady is bending her wrists and arching them up. Which makes it hard to dance with you when you do that. Either that or the guy doesn't know what he's doing. So keep the hands low, Amigos!

Now lets check out one more dance position before we move on to some of the Bachata Steps, turns, dips, and whatnot. Everything we've covered so far is more technique to make the dance feel better and help you be set up from the start to execute your moves correctly.

Don't let your hands float up like this

Palm to Palm Bachata Hold

Here's another 2 handed Bachata dance hold that may come in handy when you're dancing. It's called the palm to palm hold, and you do it just like it sounds.
You get to this hold by hooking up your hands with your partners & keeping them held low. Palms together. The mans wrists are turned outward so that the back of his hands are facing behind him.

Once again make sure that the ladies hands are on top, just like in the picture. This helps the leader, lead the steps & it helps the follower feel what she should be doing.

The same as the other two hand hold, also keep the hands low.

Palm to Palm Hold, Side view

How To....Not Step On Your Partners Feet

This is the one thing most people dread about dancing, is stepping on someones feet or even worse someone stepping on yours. Well I have some good news for you. I'm going to teach you a way to keep from stepping on your partners feet and keep them off of yours too.

Here's how it works, I call the way to keep people off your feet the "4 lanes". Just like lanes on a freeway or on a street that you drive on. We'll apply this to dancing.

Think of it this way each one of your feet goes in 1 lane. So as the guy you take up 2 lanes, because you have two feet. As the Girl you also take up 2 lanes with your two feet. So flip to the next page to see the example of this and the way the feet are positioned.

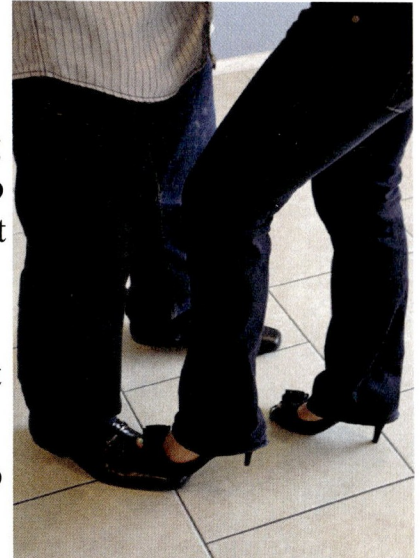

Getting stepped on

How to....Not Step on Your Partners Feet Continued

It takes all the fun out of a dance when you step on your dance partners feet or they step on yours. So a little prevention goes a long way so legs over the trick to avoiding getting stepped on & stepping on other dancers feet. It's simpler than you think, its mostly about where your feet are set up from the get go.

4 Lanes Explained:

In the photo...The **lady's right foot** is in between the mans two feet & **her left is on the outside** of his other foot.

Guys your **left foot** should be on the outside of hers and your **right foot** in between her legs.

So the idea behind this is that the mans left foot is in lane 1, the ladies right is lane 2, the mans right is lane 3, and the ladies left is in lane 4.

The feet positioned and spaced so that nobody gets stepped on

Hopefully that didn't get too confusing. So when your in the closed dance frame be sure that your feet are set up this way & it will keep you from stepping on toes. Everybody likes dancing with some one that doesn't step on their feet.

Here's a side view of a closed dance frame with the feet set up in the 4 rows. The mans left on the outside and his right is in between her two feet.

Now we've cover the basics of the Bachata dance frame & holds lets move on to more exciting things like actually dancing. So in the next section we'll cover the most important move in Bachata. The Bachata Basic!

Bachata Moves

Section # 1

Move # 1 The Bachata Basic, Two Hand Hold

0. starting position

1. Side step

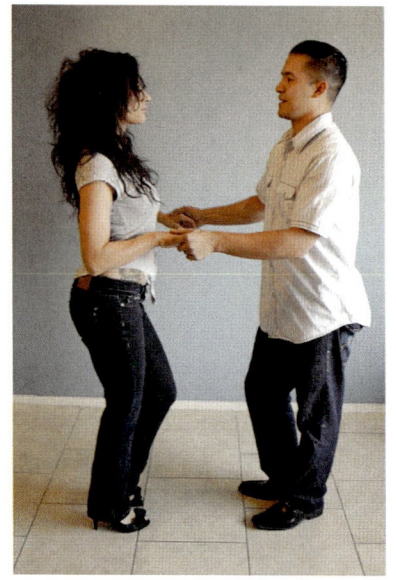

2. Step Together

3. Side Step

4. Tap foot/lift Hip

5. Side step

Style Tip: See how the dancers bend their knees in the photos, bending your knees helps loosen up your hips. Sometimes total beginners dance stiff legged. So maker sure you work those hips & legs.

Move # 1 The Bachata Basic, Two Hand Hold

6. Step Together **7. Side Step** **8. Tap/ Lift Hip**

Mans Steps Explained:

0. Start with your left foot ready.
1. Side step with your left foot.
2. Step together, Right foot
3. Side Step Left foot
4. Tap right foot, or raise right hip
5. Side step, Right foot
6. Step together, left foot
7. Side step, Right foot
8. Tap, or raise left hip

Lady's Step Explained:

0. Start with Right foot ready
1. Side step with Right Foot.
2. Step together, Left Foot.
3. Side Step, Right Foot.
4. Raise left hip, or Tap Right Foot
5. Side step, Left Foot
6. Step together, Right Foot
7. Side step, Left Foot
8. Raise right hip, or tap foot

*Each step is listed according to the beat it should be danced on. Remember Bachata basic takes 8 beats to dance & you have 8 steps, so each step/hip lift or tap takes one beat.

Move # 2 Bachata Basic (Closed Dance Frame)

0. Start position

1. Side Step

2. Step together

3. Side Step

4. Tap/Lift hip

5. Side Step

Move # 2 Bachata Basic (Closed Dance Frame) continued

6. Step Together

7. Side Step

8. Tap/lift hip

Mans Steps Explained:

0. Start with your left foot ready.
1. Side step with your left foot.
2. Step together, Right foot
3. Side Step Left foot
4. Tap right foot, or raise right hip
5. Side step, Right foot
6. Step together, left foot
7. Side step, Right foot
8. Tap, or raise left hip

Lady's Step Explained:

0. Start with Right foot ready
1. Side step with Right Foot.
2. Step together, Left Foot.
3. Side Step, Right Foot.
4. Raise left hip, or Tap Right Foot
5. Side step, Left Foot
6. Step together, Right Foot
7. Side step, Left Foot
8. Raise right hip, or tap foot

Each step or movement (hip raise or foot tap) takes only 1 beat. Take it slow and don't rush through the steps.

Move # 3 The One Armed - Bachata Basic

0. Starting position

1. Side Step

2. Step Together

3. Side Step

4. Lift Hip/ Tap

5. Side Step

Style Tip: Have your poise slightly forward to give you more of the street style look that goes well with this move. Guys have your hand over your heart and Ladies your hand on your hip or doing some sexy arm styling.

Move # 3 One Arm Bachata Basic

6. Step Together   **7. Side Step**   **8. Lift hip/tap foot**

Leaders: With the One Arm Hold you can even accentuate the beat with your right arm while your feet move to the music. Meaning as you dance your Bachata basic in the one arm hold, you can **move the arm subtly from side to side to the match the rhythm of the music**.

Mans Steps Explained:

0. Start with your left foot ready.
1. Side step with your left foot.
2. Step together, Right foot
3. Side Step Left foot
4. Tap right foot, or raise right hip
5. Side step, Right foot
6. Step together, left foot
7. Side step, Right foot
8. Tap, or raise left hip

Lady's Step Explained:

0. Start with Right foot ready
1. Side step with Right Foot.
2. Step together, Left Foot.
3. Side Step, Right Foot.
4. Raise left hip, or Tap Right Foot
5. Side step, Left Foot
6. Step together, Right Foot
7. Side step, Left Foot
8. Raise right hip, or tap foot

Move # 4 Forward & Back Basic

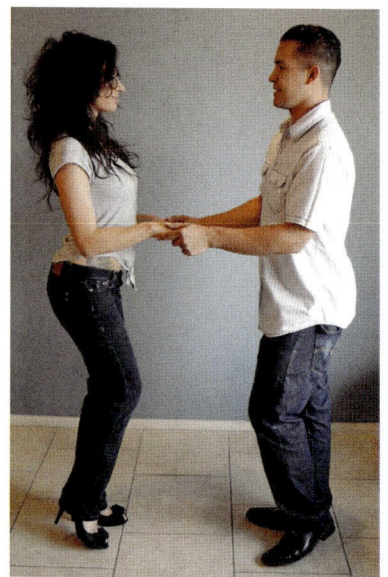
0. Two Hand Hold

1. Step

2. Together

3. Step

4. Tap/Hip Lift

5. Step

Move # 4 Forward & Back Basic

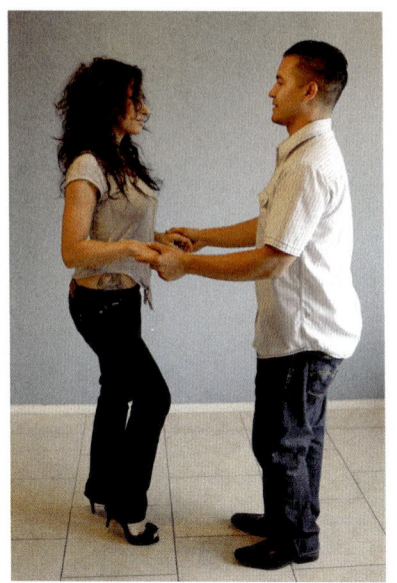  

6. Together **7. Step** **8. Tap/Hip Lift**

Stye Tip: This move can also be danced with the feet passing each other, which means, instead of stepping "together" step past your own foot. It's more style preference. Keeping your steps close together helps you appear more rhythmical, sometimes its more dynamic and exciting to really move on the dance floor by passing your feet.

Mans Steps Explained:

0. Start with your left foot ready.
1. Forward step with your left foot.
2. Step together, Right foot
3. Forward Step Left foot
4. Tap right foot, or raise right hip
5. Back step, Right foot
6. Step together, left foot
7. Back step, Right foot
8. Tap, or raise left hip

Lady's Step Explained:

0. Start with Right foot ready
1. Back step with Right Foot.
2. Step together, Left Foot.
3. Back Step, Right Foot.
4. Raise left hip, or Tap Right Foot
5. Forward step, Left Foot
6. Step together, Right Foot
7. Forward step, Left Foot
8. Raise right hip, or tap foot

Move # 5 Cross Step Basic

0. One Arm Hold

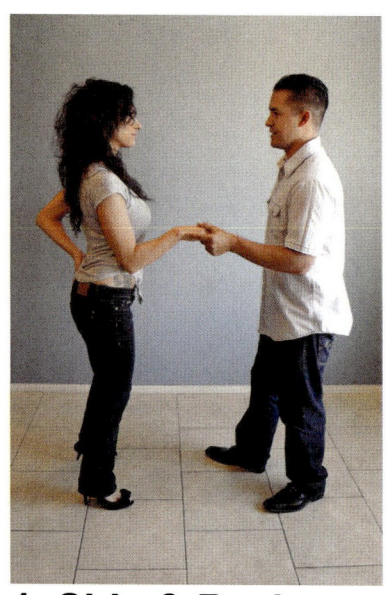
1. Side & Back

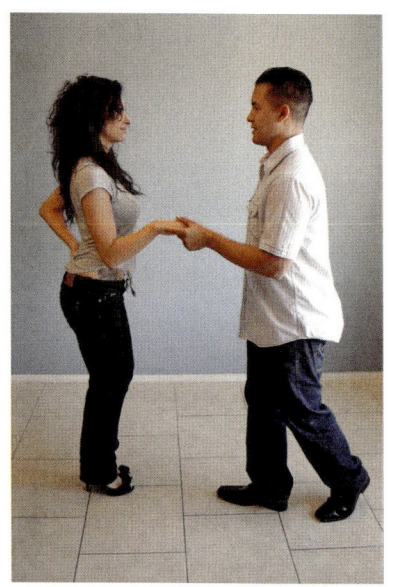
2. Cross in front

3. Side Step

4. Tap/Hip lift

5. Side & Back

Style Tip: For steps Side & Back you should take your normal side step, but have it be a smaller step & have your toes almost inline with your heel.

Move # 5 Cross Step Basic

6. Cross in Front

7. Side & Back

8. Tap/ Hip Lift

Cross Step Explained:

The "Cross Step Basic" can also be danced by the lady. Here we've demonstrated the mans steps. The ladies steps follow the same pattern of a smaller side step to begin, then crossing in front & followed up by a side step.

The Bachata "Cross Step Basic" should be done in either a "1 arm hold" like in this demo, or the 2 hand hold. Avoid doing the cross step in the "Closed Dance Frame".

Important Tip:

Your Side Steps on numbers (Counts) 1 & 5 should not be big side steps, because then it makes it harder for you to cross in front with your next step.

Move # 5 Cross Step Basic Continued (Rear View)

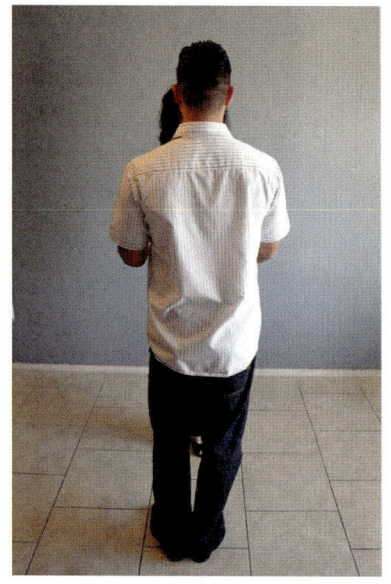

0. One arm Hold

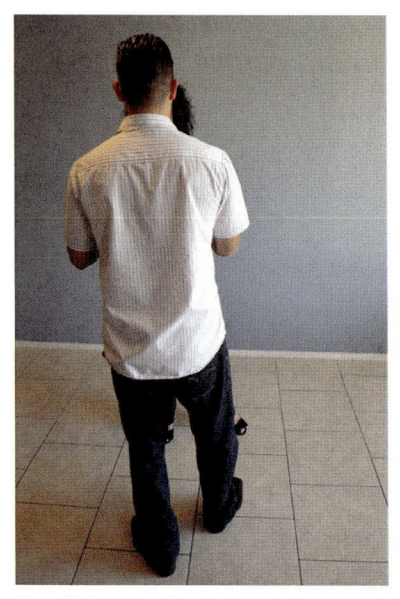

1. Side & Back

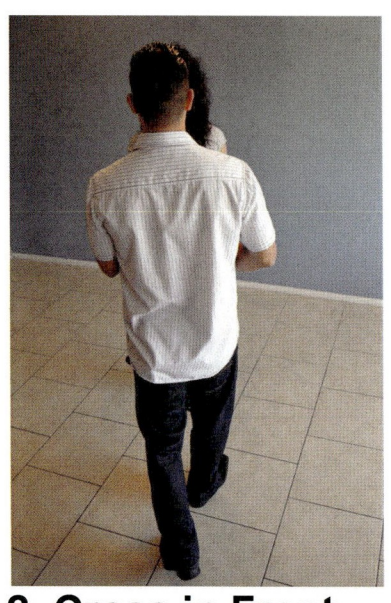

2. Cross in Front

3. Side Step

4. Tap/ Hip Lift

5. Side & Back

Move # 5 Cross Step Basic Continued (Rear View)

  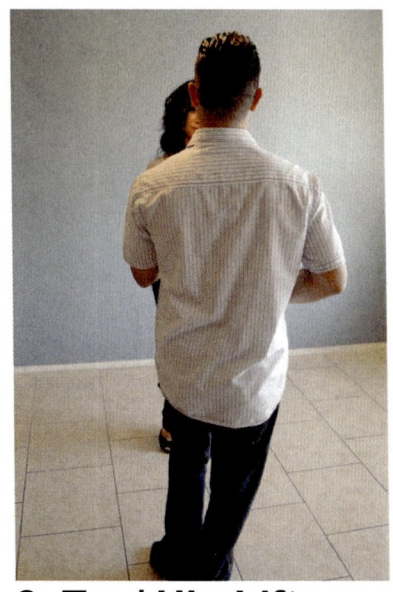

6. Cross step   **7. Side Back**   **8. Tap/ Hip Lift**

Style Tip:

If you want to add more style to the way you dance the Cross Step or any of the other steps, you can either tap with the front of your foot or tap the subtly tap the ground with your heel. You'll see Bachata dancers do one or the other, depending on how they are feeling the music and the rhythm.

So with move like the "Cross Step Basic", you can spice up the way you dance & show you partner that Latin flavor by changing up it every now and again with the exciting ways you do the basics.

Move # 6 Syncopated Bachata Basic   (Dominican Style)

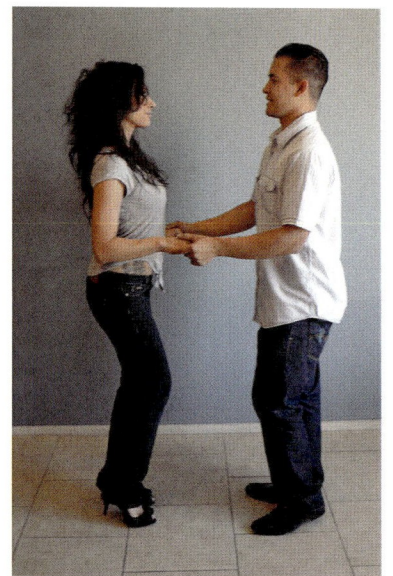
0. Two hand hold

1. Side Step

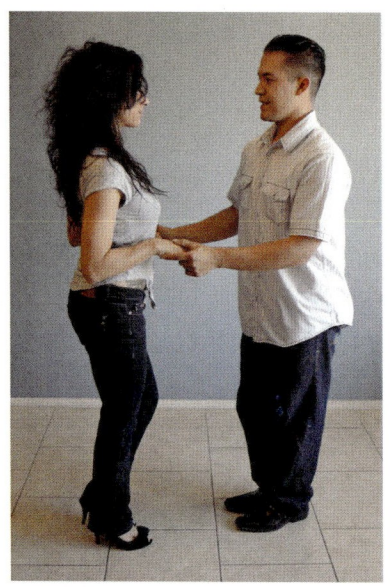
2. Together

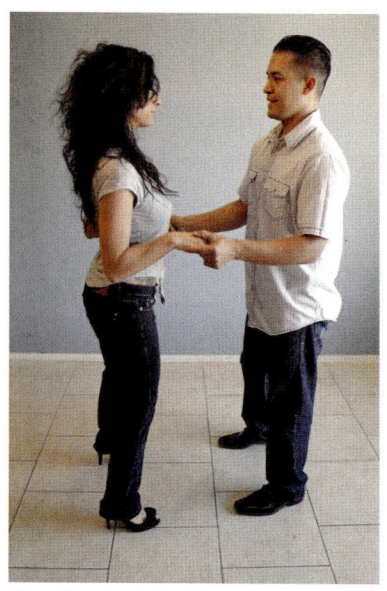
3. Side Step

4. Step behind

5. In place

Syncopated Basic Explained: You'll notice that this basic has more steps that the other Basics, but its done over the same 8 beats. Steps 4 & 5 plus 9 & 10 will be over a ½ a beat instead of a whole beat. Meaning move quicker!

Move # 6   Syncopated Basic   (Dominican Style)

6. Side Step

7. Step Together

8. Side Step

9. Step Behind

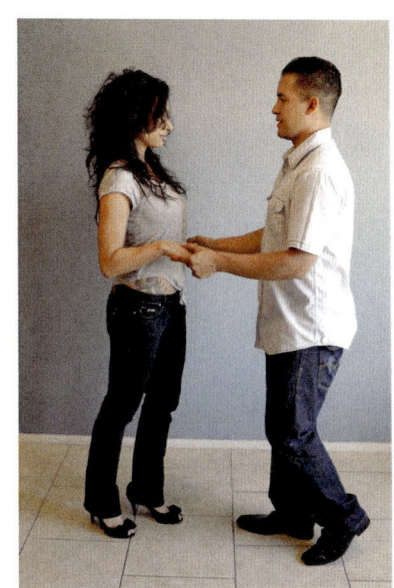
10. Step in Place

Learning tip: One way to simplify this new rhythm is to count it as "One, Two, Cha-Cha-Cha"....then back the other way, "One, Two, Cha-Cha-Cha"! Basically, with this "Dominican Style" basic you dance 10 steps over 8 beats.

Move # 7 Palm To Palm Basic

0. Starting position

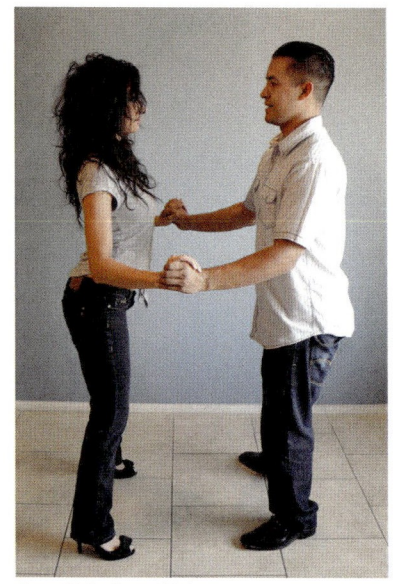
1. Side Step

2. Together

3. Side Step

4. Tap/ Hip Lift

5. Side Step

Beginner Tip: Remember not to squeeze down on your partners hands.

Move # 7 Palm to Palm Basic

6. Together   **7. Side Step**   **8. Tap/Hip Lift**

Mans Steps Explained:

0. Start with your left foot ready.
1. Side step with your left foot.
2. Step together, Right foot
3. Side Step Left foot
4. Tap right foot, or raise right hip
5. Side step, Right foot
6. Step together, left foot
7. Side step, Right foot
8. Tap, or raise left hip

Lady's Step Explained:

0. Start with Right foot ready
1. Side step with Right Foot.
2. Step together, Left Foot.
3. Side Step, Right Foot.
4. Raise left hip, or Tap Right Foot
5. Side step, Left Foot
6. Step together, Right Foot
7. Side step, Left Foot
8. Raise right hip, or tap foot

Sensual Bachata Stying

Section #2

Sexy Hair Comb Loop

This is a sexy technique called Hair comb, which can be described as looping yours and your partners hands around either your head or hers. This is a sensual and seductive type move that really can spice up a dance. Here we have an up close look of the loop/hair comb.

Mans Right Palm Facing Up, and his wrist bent at a 90 degree angle. Have the ladies hand on top of your with her finger tips on yours. The further apart your palm is from hers the more room you'll have to loop her with this move.

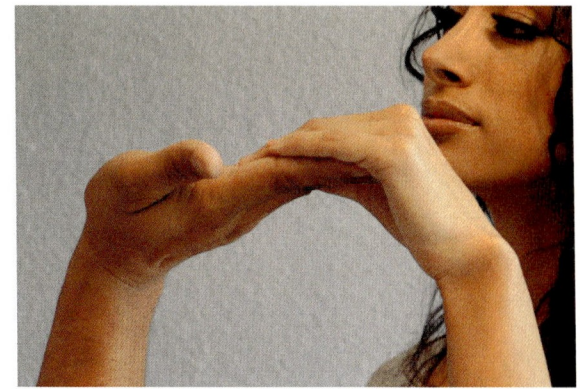

Raise your arm slowly and smoothly and look at her through the opening of the two arms while you do this. So that the lady doesn't think its a turn or a spin. Sometimes newer female dancers will mistake your raising her arm as a turn. So take 2-3 beats just to raise her arm.

Gently loop the arm behind her head, watch carefully so you don't mess up her hair in the process.

Ladies: When the man releases this hold be sure to lower your arm and do some sexy arm styling until he takes you into another dance hold.

Sexy Hair Comb/Loop (Side View)

Mans Palm up

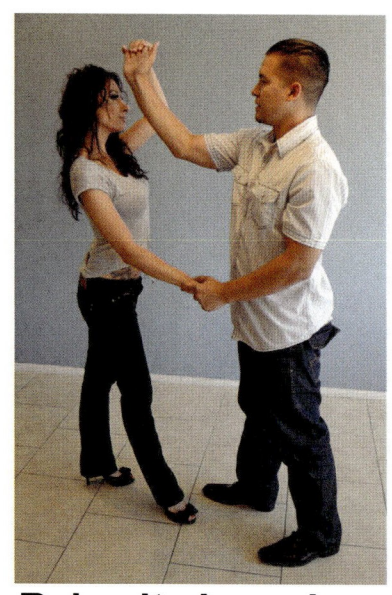
Raise it above her

Loop the girls hair

Ladies, Once the man neck loops or hair combs you be sure that your elbow isn't point out to your left, instead have it pointing forward, then slowly lower your arm to the next move.

Beginner Tip: I teach new guys to think how a waiter carries a tray, with his palm up and fingers flat. This is the trick behind making this move work. Like anything it takes practice.

Mans Neck Loops (Right Arm)

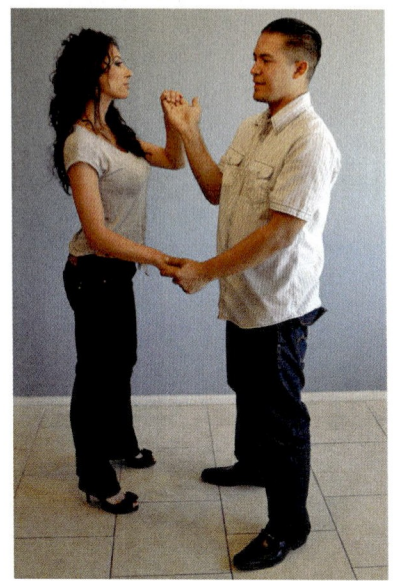

1. Right Palm up

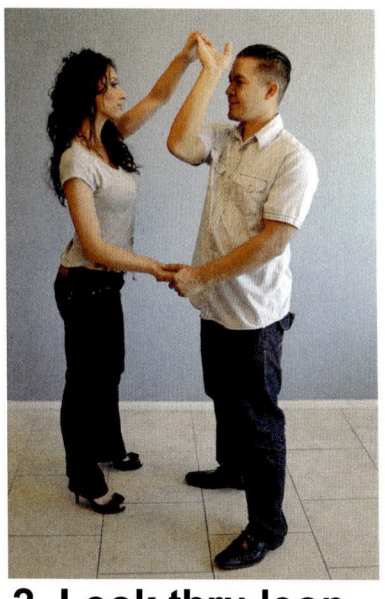

2. Look thru loop

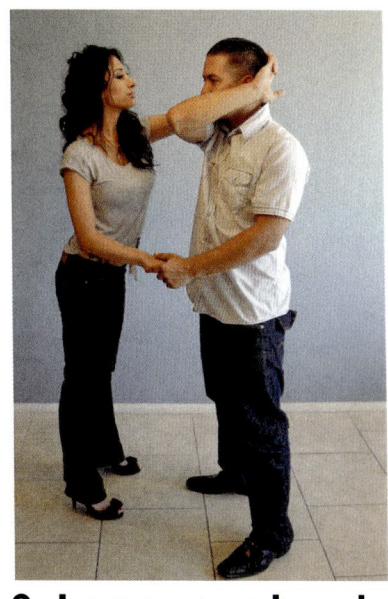

3. Loop your head

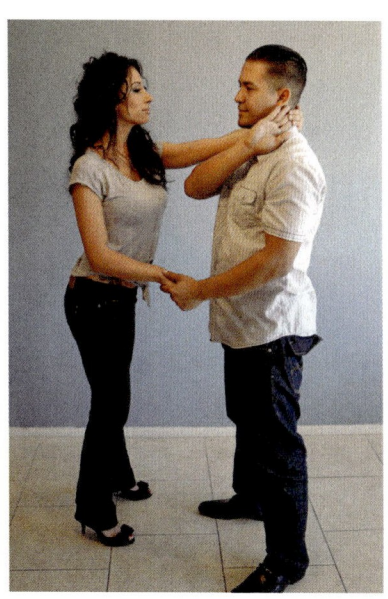

4. Keep the Hold

Beginner Tip: I suggest beginner learn this move by practicing the arms first, before combining it with the feet step. Once you can do this move easily then try it while doing the basic.

Mans Neck Loop (Left Arm)

1. Mans Palm Up

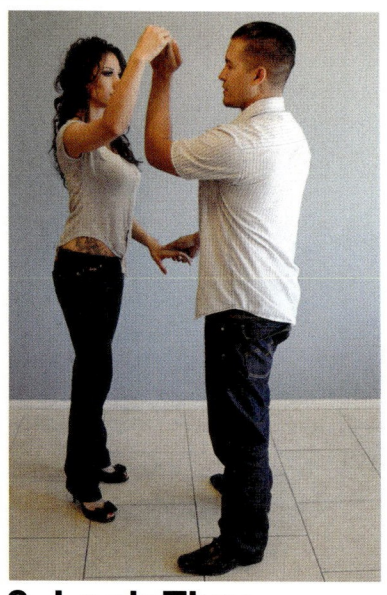
2. Look Thru

3. Loop your head

4. Finish Hold

Beginner Tip: This move should not mess up your hair, the wrap should pass around your head without touching your hair. A trick to making this work is only having a "finger tip" type hold with both hands.

Move # 8 Mans Neck Loop & Basic

0. Mans palm up

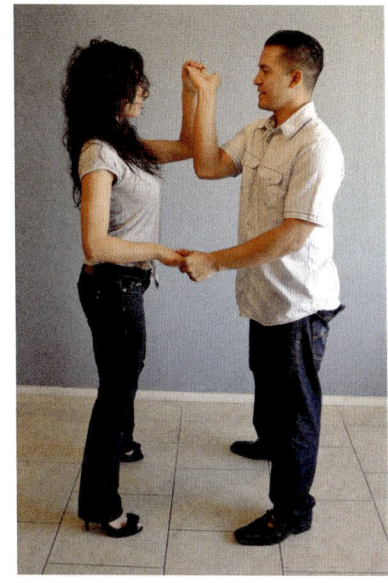
1. Raise arm

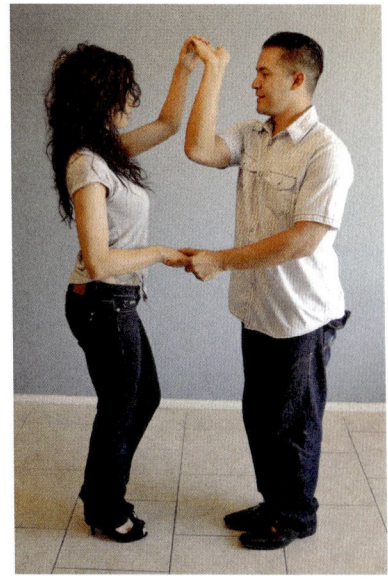
2. look Thru

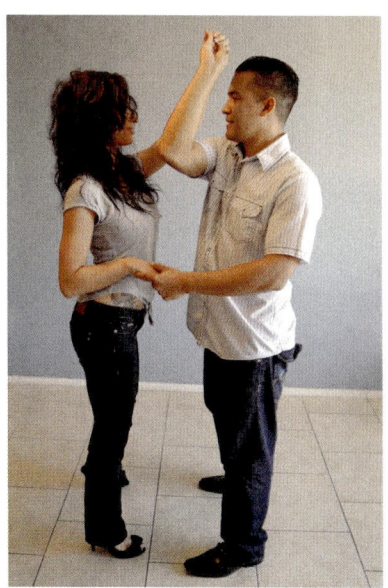
3. Start loop

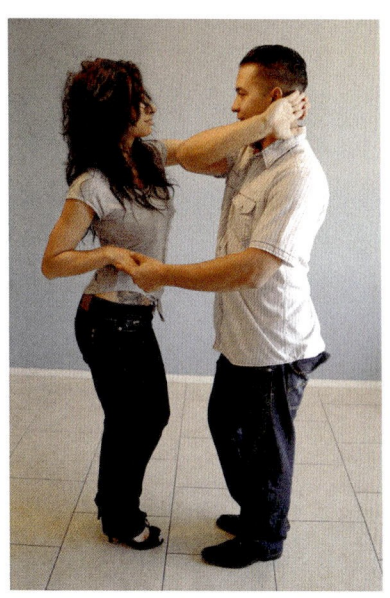
4. Loop Head

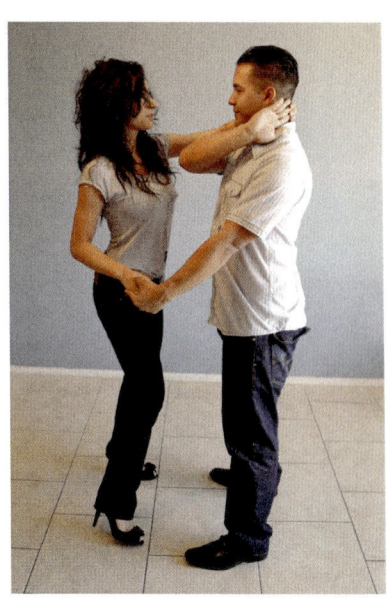
5. Keep hold

Style Tip: Neck loops should be done slowly & sensually, don't rush to "loop" your self. Take your time with these loops & do it over 2-3 beats. Remember Bachata is a Sexy & Romantic dance. We want our movements to resemble this.

Move # 8 Mans Neck Loop & Basic

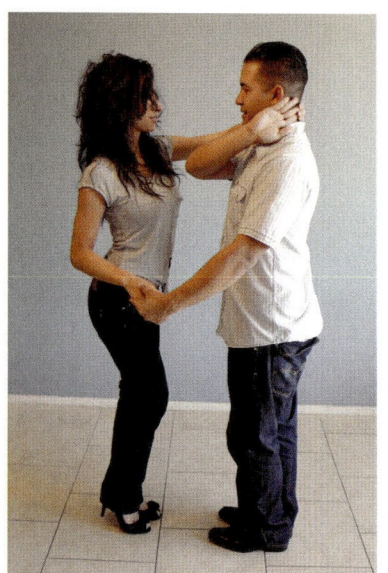 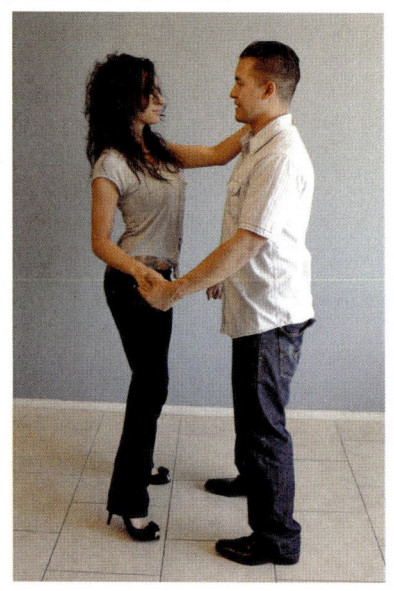 

6. Keep Hold **7. Release loop** **8. Closed frame**

Style Tip: Ladies, when the man lets go of this wrap, keeping your arm there and slowly lowering it, as well as slowly caressing his neck & shoulder with your hand on the way to the closed dance frame add more sex appeal and style to the move.

The mans & Ladies steps for the Bachata basic and Neck Loop are the exact same as the regular basic.

Next, we'll cover the "**2 arm wrap**" another looping type move that is similar to this style of trick. Then later in the book when we cover turns and other techniques I'll show ways to end certain moves with a neck loop or wrap. This will give you ideas on how to combine your Bachata moves on the dance floor.

Two Arm Neck Wraps/ Loop, Explained

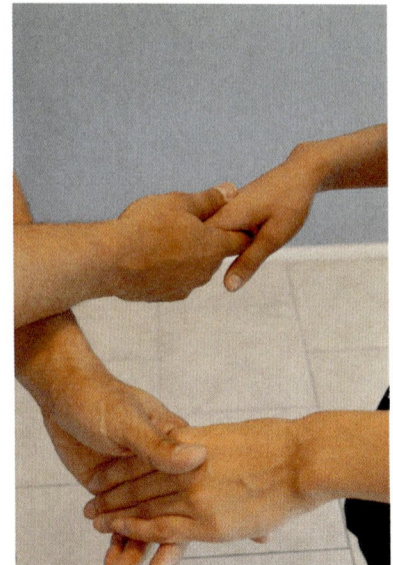
0. Cross Hold

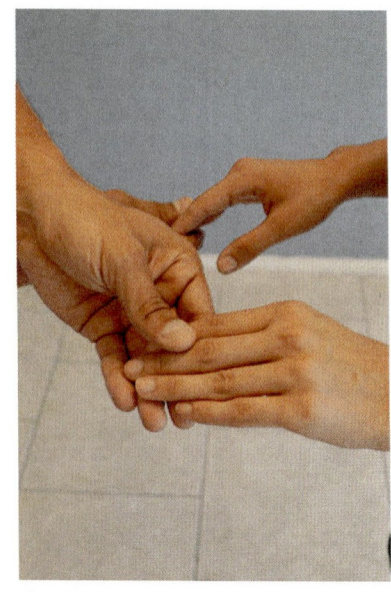
1. Finger Tip Hold

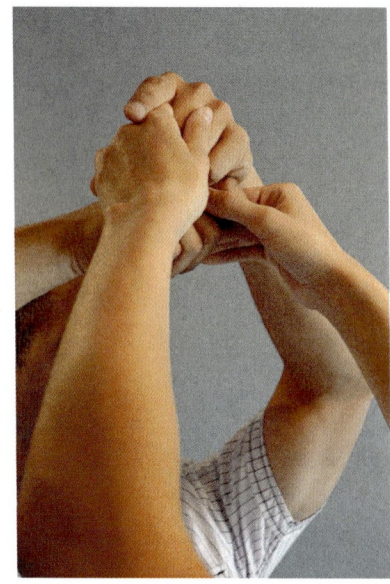
3. Raise Arms

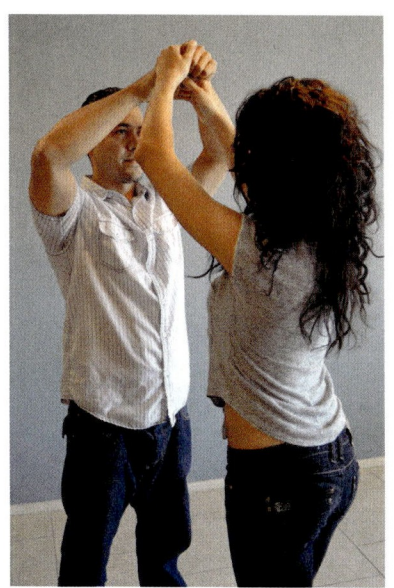
4. Look Thru

5. Lower Arms

6. Complete

First we started this move in the "Cross Hand Hold" that's when the mans arms are crossed like an x and so are the ladies. This is a common hold you'll be using & so doing this wrap will give you a spicy way to end certain moves. Next we'll cover how to use this with the foot steps.

Move # 9   Mans 2 Arm Wrap & Basic

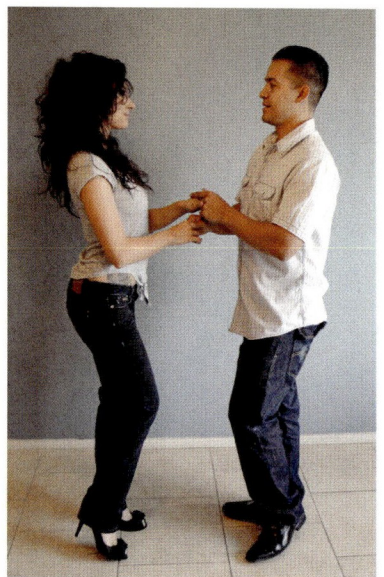
0. Cross arm hold

1. Raise Arms

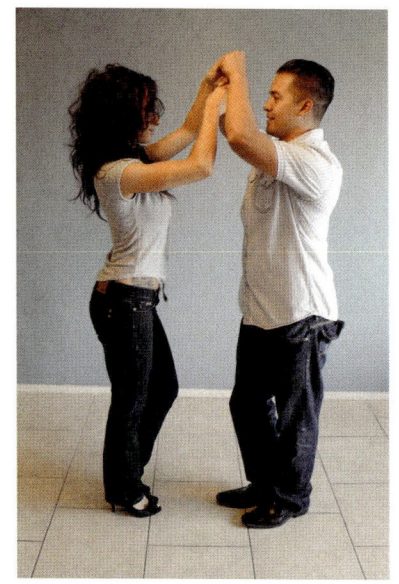
2. Higher

3. Behind head

4. Drop to neck

5. Go to Frame

The Steps for the mans & Lady is the same as in Move # 1 The Bachata Basic. So Before learning this move, be sure that you know the basic.

Move # 9   Mans 2 Arm Wrap & Basic

6. Side

7. Together

8. Side Step

9. Tap/ Hip Lift

Important tip: In this example we started with the mans left hand crossed over his right, this move will work with the right hand on top as well. These cross arm hold are easy once you get the hang of it and these loops & wraps add extra style and pizazz to the dance.

2 Neck loop the lady

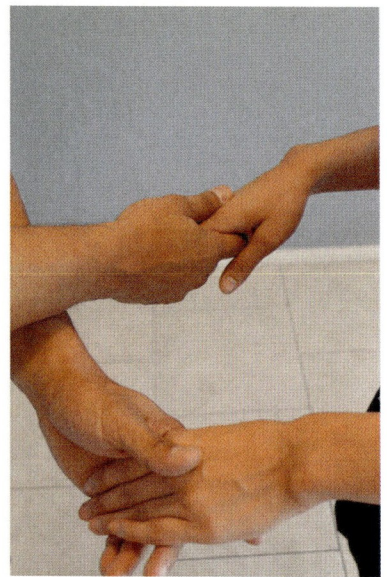
0. Arms Crossed

1. Raise Arms slowly

2. Lift over her

3. Lower hands

4. Follow thru

Ladies: Keep your arms relaxed and loose through out this move and try not to resist it or pull your hands away because if you do either it kills the move.

Guys: Do the move slowly & Gently, and don't mess up her hair.

Finish this move by getting into a 2 hand hold or Closed Dance Frame.

Bachata Turns

Section #3

Move # 10 The Man Turn

0. One Arm Hold

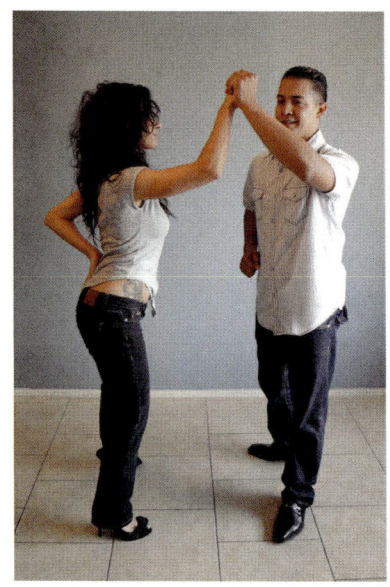
1. Raise arm/side step

2. Step under

3. Side step

4. Tap

5. Side step

Beginner Tip: An important detail here is that the man opens and closes his left hand to make the turn easier on his partners wrist. If you just keep your hand clamped down on hers you twist her wrist in some really uncomfortable ways. So open you hands midway and keep a gentle hold with the hands.

Bachata Move # 10 The Man Turn

6. Step Together   **7. Side Step**   **8. Tap/ Hip Lift**

Guys Steps: On this step the man turns to his **left**. So you'll be turning counter clockwise. One other important tip is that your foot steps should be left, right, left.

Beginner Tips: Guys, be sure to **raise your arm above your own head** and not your partners, so keep the hands more on your side. This way she doesn't think you want her to turn.

Also, Guys as you take your first step on your left foot, look through the raised arm in the direction your going. As if you were spotting.

Ladies: When the man turns himself you should do the basic step, and keep up with him as he moves to the side just like you normally would when you dance a Basic, which is shown on Move # 1.

Style Tip: The lady can keep her hand on her hip, or back hip like in pics. Once you learn the ladies arm styling you can then do a "hair comb" or other sexy and stylish moves.

Move # 11 Ladies Outside Turn

0. One arm Hold

1. Lift arm/Open hand

2. Outward turn

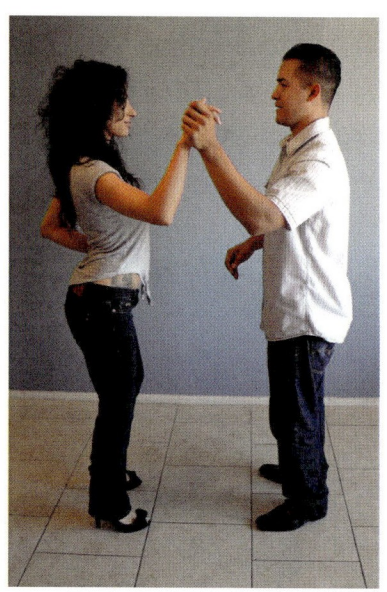
3. Lowering hand

4. One arm basic

5. Side step

Leading Tip: Be sure to wind up or prep this move before the first beat so that the lady has enough time to prepare to turn. If you wait for the first beat to do this, its already to late. So before any turn prep/wind up so she knows.

Move # 11 Ladies Outside Turn continued

6. Step Together

7. Side Step

8. Tap or Hip

Ladies: This is a 3 Step turn, the first step with your right foot gets you going to the side, the second you turn your back to the guy, and third swing around to face your partner and finish with the "One Arm Bachata Basic".

Ladies Outside Turn Steps Explained:

1. Side Step & start rotating to your right
2. Do a ½ a turn to your right & step on your left foot.
3. Do a ½ a turn to your right, again stepping on your right foot.
4. Face your partner, raise your hip or mark the beat with a tap & continue with a basic to the side.

Beginner Tip: When we do turn we want to keep our steps small, both the leader and follower. This isn't waltz where we try to travel around the dance floor. Especially in a busy night club. Try to almost turn in place.

Move # 12 Ladies Inside Turn & Neck Loop

0. Prep lady for turn

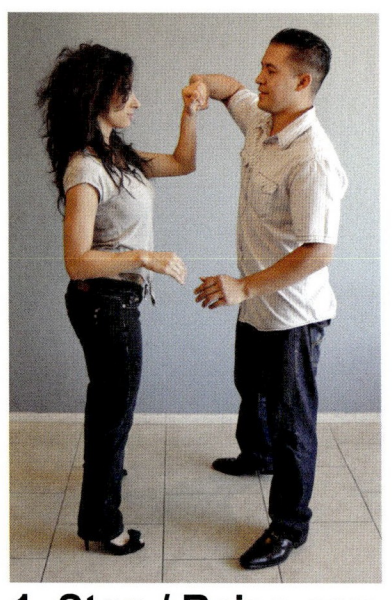
1. Step / Raise arm

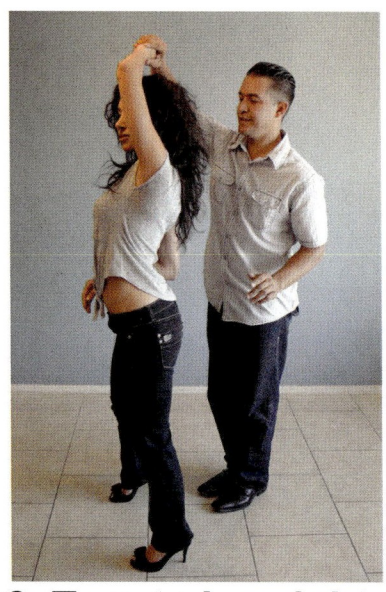
2. Turn to her right

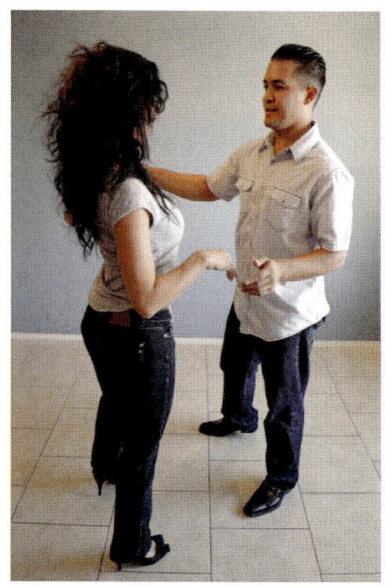
3. Face partner

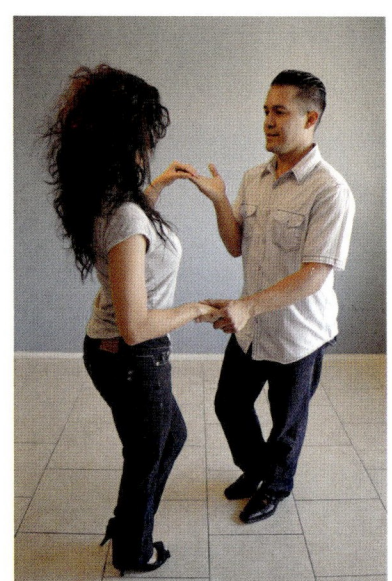
4. Tap/hip Raise hand

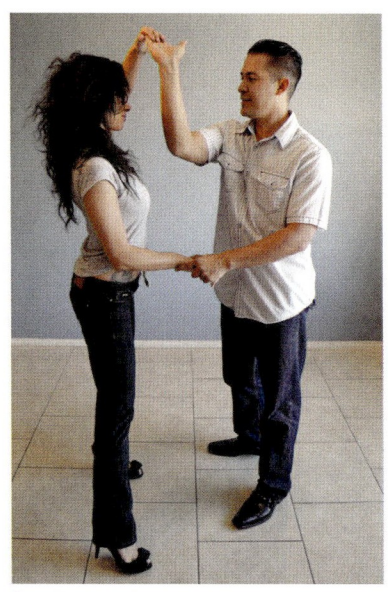
6. Look thru loop

Beginner tip: Leaders remember to start raising the hand before first step so that she know in advance that your about to turn her. With this turn you'll also have to open and close your hand grip so that she can turn easily.

Move # 12 Ladies Inside Turn & Neck Loop

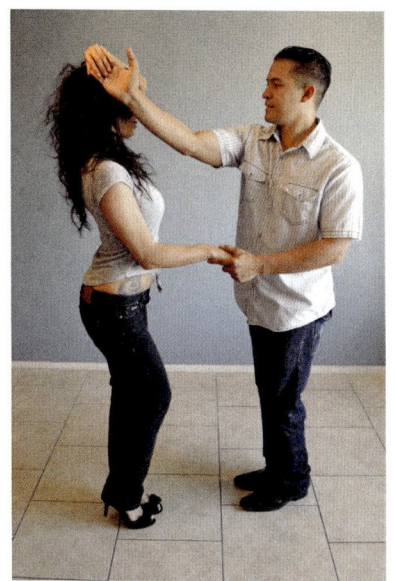
6. Together/ Loop her

7. Finish Loop

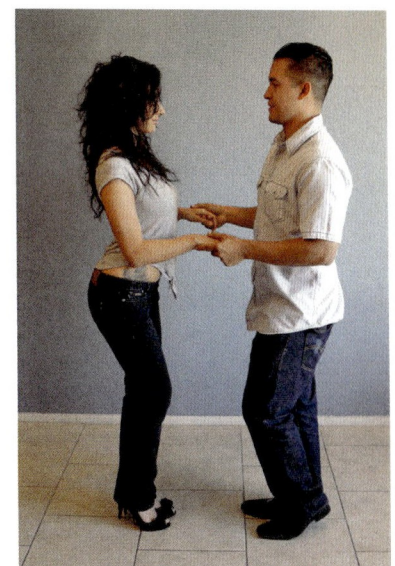
8. Lower into hold

This is a combination of 2 moves, the **inside turn** and a **1 armed loop**. Just like the one's you learned earlier in the book where you loop yourself or her.

You can also just do the Inside turn half of this combo and finish it off with the last 4 steps of the Bachata basic. Which of course are shown earlier in this book.

Beginner Tip: The ladies inside turn in led with the mans Right arm, and it brought across her face to help lead her to her right side. You have to give the girl enough lead so that she knows its a turn and that she follows through with her steps.

Remember to do the Neck loops slowly, this makes them more sensual and if you do them slow and smooth like Rico Suave, she wont think your trying to turn or spin her, which can mess up this combo.

Ladies: You can decide when to break away from the loop by letting go, then follow it by lowering your arm/hand in a sexy way. See the ladies arm styling section later in the book.

Move # 13   Ladies Inside Turn   w/ Mans Left Arm

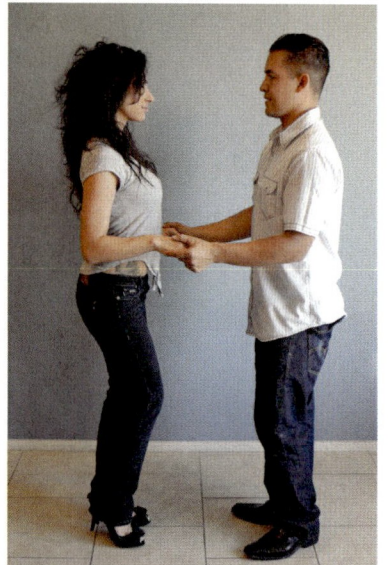
0. Two hand hold

1. Side Step

2. Together

3. Side Step

4. Tap/ Prep turn

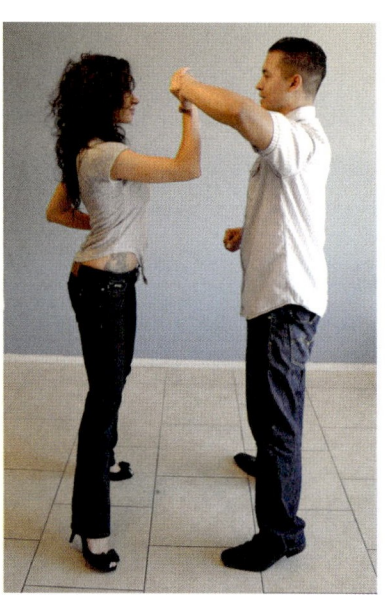
5. Side & start turn

Beginner Tip: Notice that when the man turns the Lady his foot step stay the same as in the Bachata Basic.

Also you can see in **#4** that the man "flips" his hand hold to turn her easier.

Move # 13 Ladies Inside Turn   w/ Mans Left Arm

6. Together/ Turn　　　**7. Face each other**　　　**8. Tap/Hip Lift**

Beginner Tip, For Ladies: At a beginner level the lady can keep her Right hand on her hip as the man turns her. Wait until he offer to bring you back into the frame, or one of the other hold.

You don't want to start reaching or grabbing for his hands. This looks needy and it can throw off the guy. So either keep it on your hip or once you've learned some arm styling feel free to do a hair comb to your self or some other feminine styling.

Move # 14 The Cradle

0. Two Hand Hold

1. Side Step

2. Together

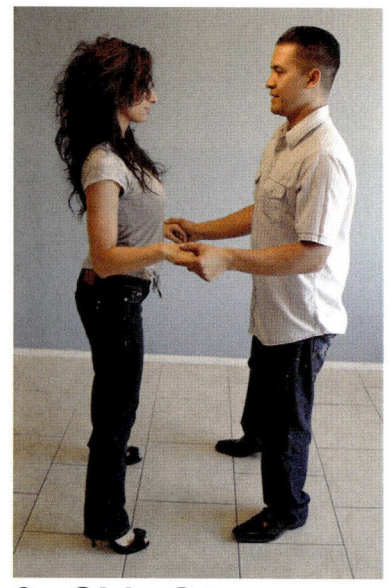

3. Side Step

4. Tap/ Prep Turn

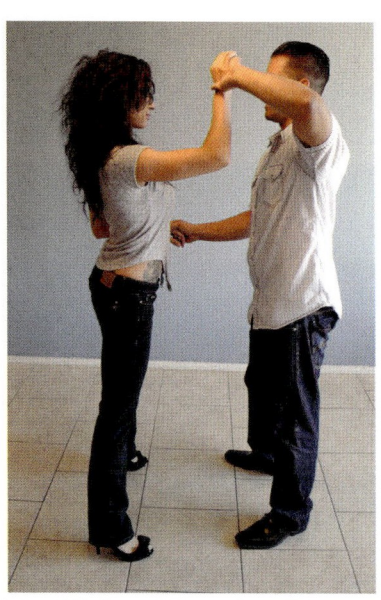

5. Side Begin Turn

Lead Technique: Notice the different hand holds for count 4 & 5, this helps guide the lady inward for the Cradle hold. Also guys your right hand (the lower one) can help with the lead by guiding to turn outward.

Move # 14 The Cradle

6. Turning

7. Lower arms

8. Hip or Tap

1. Raise mans left arm

2. Unwind her

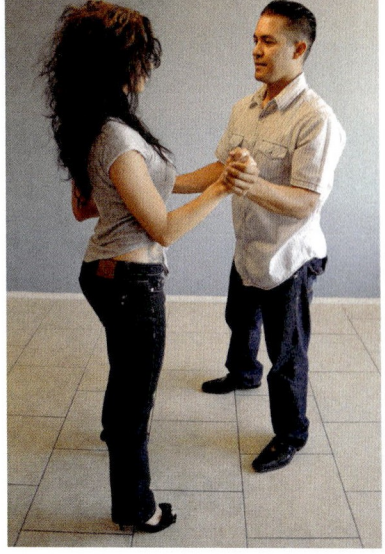
3. Side step

Beginner Tip: The ladies turn into the cradle should take 3 steps, **Left-Right-Left** then she taps or does a hip movement and exits with **Right-Left-Right**. Be sure that you step down all three times and get the tap or hip in, sometimes newer dancers hold one beat and only take 2 steps which get them of the rhythm and right foot work.

Move # 14   The Cradle (Continued)

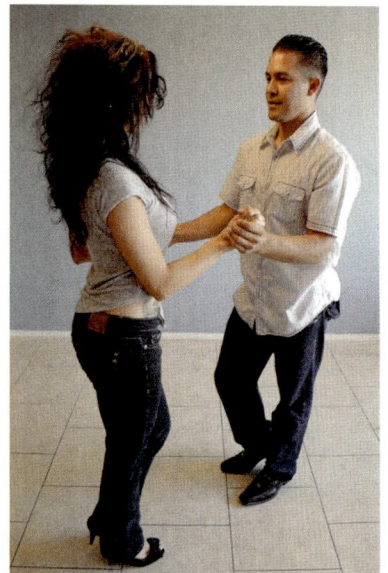
4. Tap/ Hip Lift

5. Side Step

6. Step Together

7. Side Step

8. Tap or Hip

Learning Tip: I recommend beginner first learn the arms correctly, how to wrap the lady in a cradle and how to take her out. Then combine it with the foot steps.

Style Tip: Also you can stay in the cradle hold & dance a full basic (8 beats) with the lady wrapped up *then* release her and do the basic, like shown here.

Ladies Hammer Locks

Section # 4

Move # 15 Hammer Lock (to Left)

0. Two Hand Hold

1. *Split the Arms

2. Start the Turn

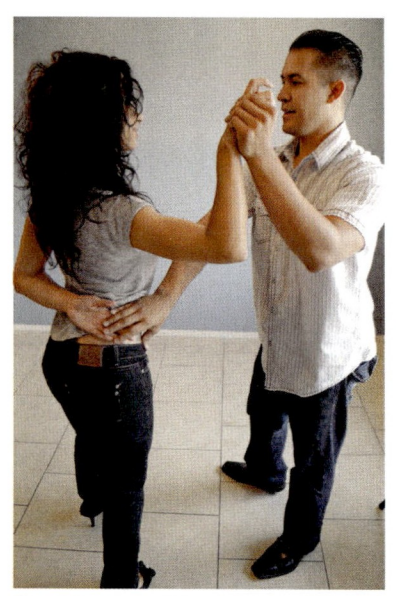

3. Face Partner

4. Tap/Hip Lift

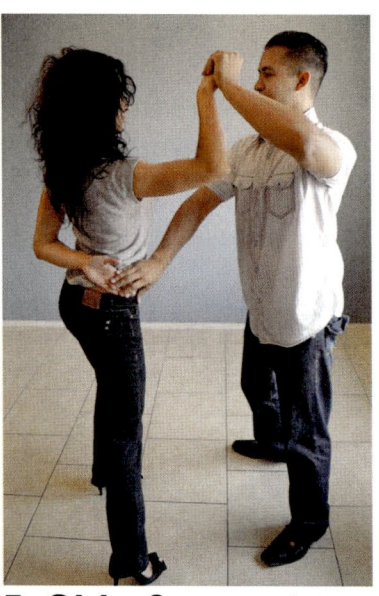

5. Side & prep turn

Split the Arms: This is when the man **Raises** his **left hand** & **Lowers** his **Right hand**, I call this splitting the arms. In this case right hand should be pressed down gently & Raise the left just above the ladies head.

57

Move # 15 Hammer Lock (to left) Continued...

6. Turn

7. Side Step

8. Tap lower hands

Ladies Turn Explained: The lady does a 3 step Turn, just like in the "Outside turn" that is shown earlier in the book, but with the "Hammer-Lock" the man keeps hold of both of the ladies hands.

As the lady your steps for the turn are: **Right-Left-Right** then face your partner with your body...and either tap your foot or raise your Hip. Make sure that you are turning to <u>your right</u>.

When the mans <u>Turns you out</u> your steps are: **Left-Right-Left** this is done by turning to your left...and then tap or do your hip.

On the next page we'll go over some tricks and tips to making the hammer-Lock work and things to avoid.

Hammer Lock Beginner tips:

Hand Hooks: If the Ladies hand slips away from your grip it means that you'll need to curl your fingers like small hooks, just like in the photo to the right. Keep it gentle and don't dig your nails into your partners hand.

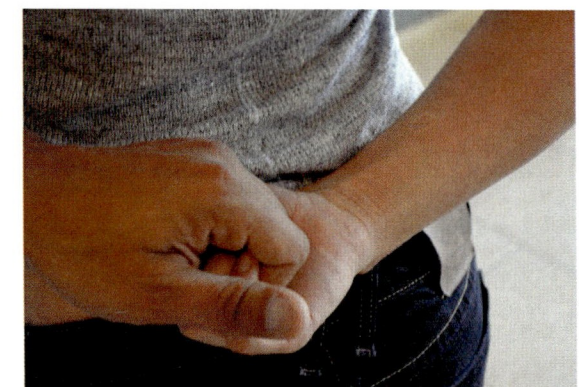

Press the Hip: When you lead the hammer-Lock the girl should be facing you with *her body* on the 4th beat. If she doesn't press on the front of her hip with your right hand, when you do the Hammer Lock to the left. And just reverse it when your doing one to the right.

Pressing on her hip helps "square her up" with you or not facing you, if she's "under turning". This is a technique to use on newer Bachata girls. If she already know these moves then you don't have to "Press the Hip".

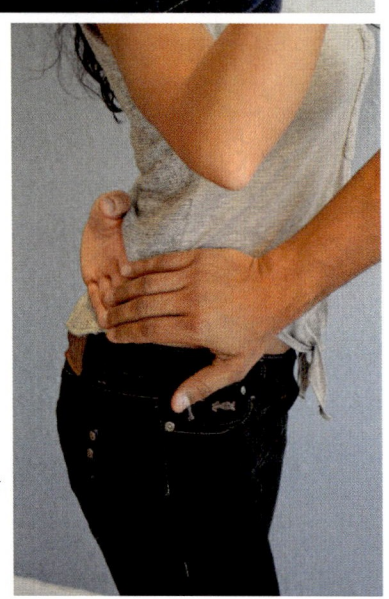

Chicken Wing Arm: This is when girls arm is bent like a chicken wing when your doing a hammer lock. This is a beginner mistake and something you want to avoid.

Ladies: With the hammer lock you want your arm at either a 90 degree angle or lower if the man straightens it out. Also avoid having your right arm Hyper extended or "locked out".

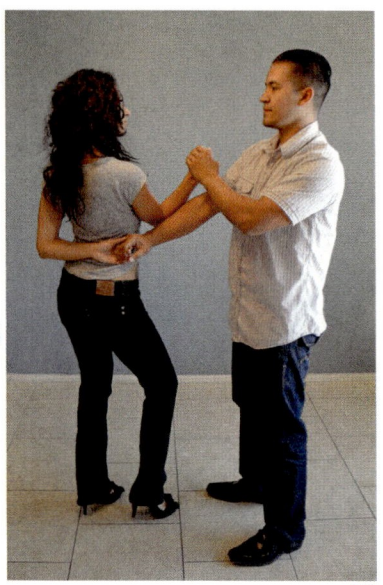

Hammer Lock Beginner Tips

Guys: Usually I teach beginner dancers to keep their arm at a 90 degree angle when they do a hammer-Lock because its easier to prep the turns to get the lady out of the move among other benefits.

The picture on the side shows the **girls arm straightened** which is also a **styling technique** that you can add to the way you dance the Bachata Hammer-Locks. Remember that when your going to turn her raise your hand in time to give her a prep so that she knows ahead.

Practice the Arms: For an experienced dancer the hammer lock is a simple move. When your first trying it out it can be confusing so I have new dancers practice putting their arms in the position.

Here she has her left arm behind her back and her we have her right arm at a 90 degree angle. This is the position that we come to in the Hammer lock to the mans left.

Now that you have a better idea of how to do a Hammer Lock to the left lets look at some of the other Hammer Lock variations like the Hammer lock to the right & the mans hammer lock.

Move # 16 Hammer Lock (to the Right)

0. Two Hand Hold

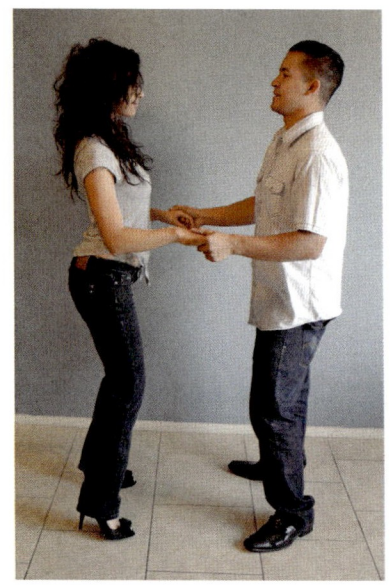
1. Side Step

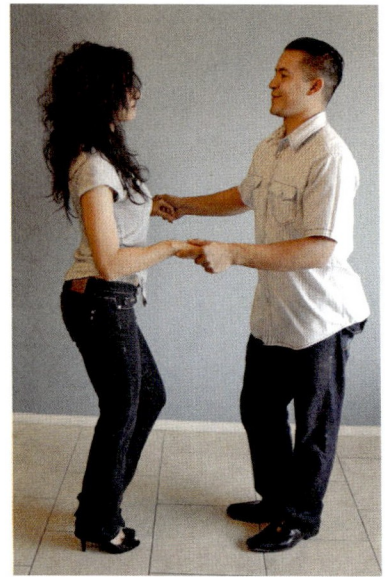
2. Together

3. Side Step

4. Tap & prep turn

5. *Split Hands

Split Hands: The leader Raises his Right hand palm up & lowers his left hand while keeping a finger tip hold with his partner. So its like your splitting them, one raises the other lowers.

Move # 16 Hammer Lock (To the Right) Continued

6. ½ Turn Her left

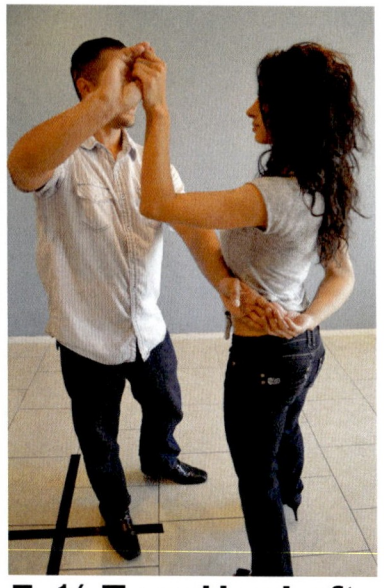
7. ½ Turn Her Left

8. Hip or Tap

1. Side Step

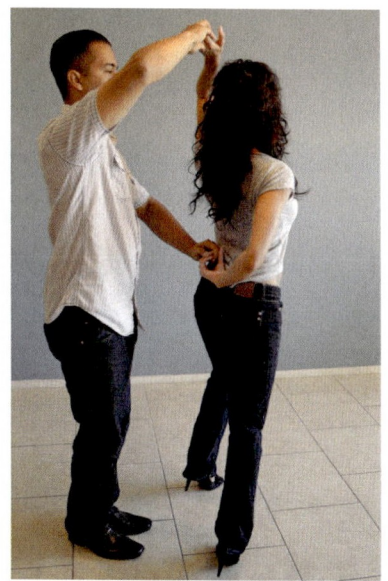
2. ½ Turn Her Right

3. ½ Turn Her Right

Beginner Tip: This move begins with 1 thru 4 of the Bachata basic, then we start the Hammer Lock to the right.

Move # 16   Hammer Lock to the Right (Continued)

4. Hip or Tap

Finish: With either a ½ a Bachata Basic to the side or the man can lead a 1 arm neck loop like we show earlier in the book. Or you can even neck loop the lady and transition from here.

So far we've covered a Hammer Lock to the Left & one to the right. In the next section we'll learn A Hammer Lock for the Guys, this move is more on the intermediate to advanced level but don't let it discourage you. But like anything make sure to learn your basics first and take your time with the steps and you'll be dancing more difficult moves before you know it.

Beginner tip: Hammer lock to the right, refers to **the mans right side** & Hammer Lock to the left, refers to **the mans Left hand side**.

Mans Hammer-Lock

Move # 17 Mans Hammer Lock & Dip under Combo

0. Two Hands Hold

1. Side Step

2. Together

3. Side Step

4. Tap or Hip

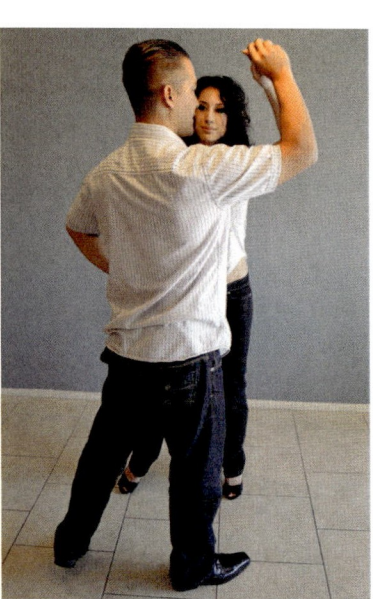

5. Split Hands & Side

Beginner Tips: This move begins with the first 4 Steps of the "Basic" then the man raise his Right Arm & lowers his left and does a 3 step turn to his right. With each step doing a ½ turn rotation.

Move # 17 Mans Hammer Lock & Duck under Combo

6. ½ Turn mans Right

7. ½ Turn Mans Right

8. Hip & Prep Loop

1. Side

2. Together & Loop her

3. Side & Keep Loop

Beginner Tip: Notice how the man fold his right arm behind his back but still keeps his fingers connected to her hand. See the section on hammer locks to get a closer look at the finger hook technique.

Move # 17 Mans Hammer Lock & Duck under Combo

4. Release right arm

5. Bend Knees

6. Duck Head Under

7. Raise up

8. Tap & Finished

Ladies: You have the easy part, when the man does these steps just do your Bachata Basic of Side-together-Side. This move is designed to not interrupt your steps and your rhythm. It may throw you off the first time someone does this move, but just keep dancing your steps and moving those hips.

Turns & Combo's

Section # 5

Move # 18 Mans Waist Turn

0. Two Hand Hold

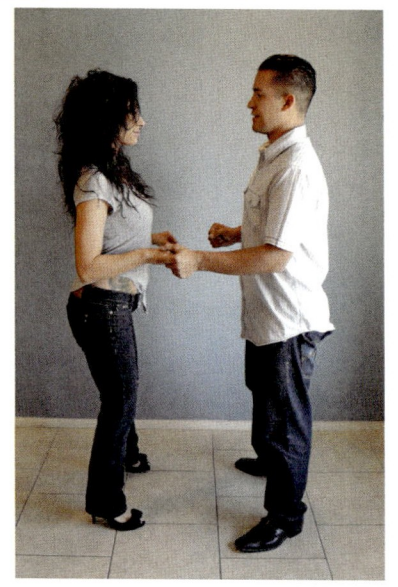
1. Release right hand

2. ½ Turn- keep hold

3. ½ Turn to right

4. Tap or Hip

5. Side Step

Ladies: Let your hand caress across his midsection as he turns this add more sensuality and give it the true Bachata feel.

Guys: Turn "into" her hand, release your grip, and leave it on your body.

Move # 18 Mans Waist Turn

6. Step Together   **7. Side Step**   **8. Tap or Hip**

Beginner Tip: On this move the man is turning to his left, counter clockwise. You do a ½ a turn for each beat. Keep your steps small so the lady doesn't have to run to keep up with you turning. Like always look in the direction that you turn. This will give you better technique and it will improve your style too.

This move is also a great one to do if the girl doesn't know how to turn and you want to do something fancy beyond just the basics. Or if your want to vary things up a bit and add in a turn for yourself.

Ladies: On this type of move you can dance your regular steps of the basic and once you advance you can start adding in styling and syncopated ("Dominican style" steps) to keep it fun & interesting.

Move # 19 Behind the Back, Hand Switch

0. One Arm Hold

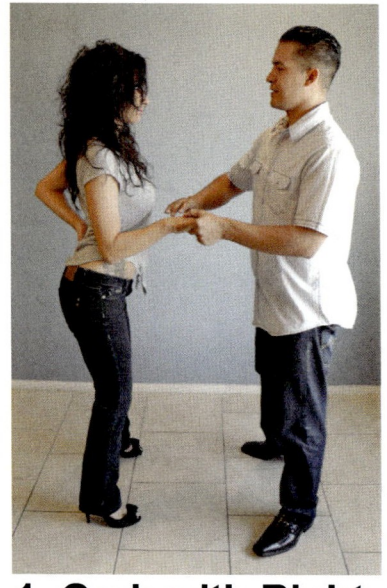
1. Grab with Right

2. Still Right hand

3. Switch to left hand

Face partner (3rd beat)

4. Tap or Hip Lift

Beginner Tip: In photo #3 it shows the man switching her hand behind his back, he lets go with his **right hand** and takes hold with his **left**. Then you finish the basic in the One arm hold, just like when you started the move.

Move # 19 Behind the Back Hand Switch

5. Side Step

6. Step Together

7. Side Step

8. Tap or Hip Lift

This behind the back move doesn't require much flexibility, so don't be intimidated. If you can touch your arms behind your back then you can do this Bachata move. Practicing this move will help you develop this skill & having your turn down already is also a must when learning this move.

Move # 20 Cross Hand Turns (mans Right over Left)

0. Right over Left

1. Side & Start Turn

2. ½ Turn Lady

3. ½ Turn-face partner

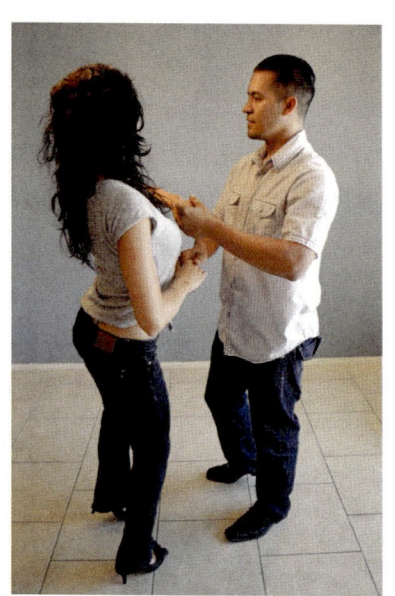

4. Hip or Tap

5. Side & Prep turn

Ladies: "Spot", or look in the direction that the man is turning you. This give you more style and it keeps him from accidentally running you into some other couple on the dance floor. Because you can see where your going.

Move # 20 Cross Hand Turns (Mans Right over Left)

6. ½ Turn Lady

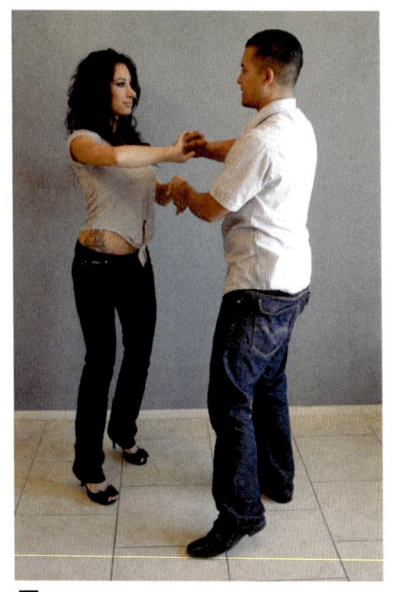
7. ½ Turn face partner

8. Tap or Hip

Cross Hand Turns Explained: In this move we turn the lady twice, first to the mans left keeping the 2 hand hold, but opening up your hand hold so she can turn with out you mangling her wrists.

The we turn her to the mans right side, back to where we started. We keep hold of both hands but open them up and change our hand connection so that we can lead her and so she can turn comfortably.

With this move the man starts with his right hand over his left and at the end of this move this is also the hand position that you'll finish in.

Hand Shake with One Under: The easiest way to get into this move, by getting a "hand shake" with your partner, your **right hand** to hers. Then with the other hand, **your left**, reach *under* the hand shake and get her other hand.

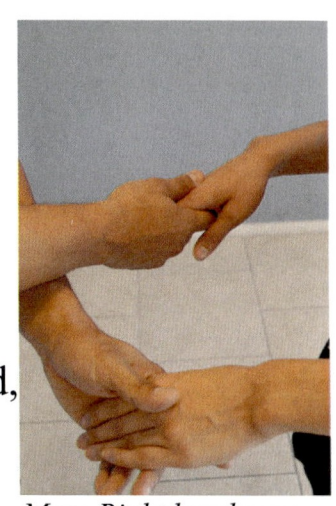
Mans Right hand over his Left

Move # 21 Mans Inside Turn-Loop & Waist Wrap

0. Two Hand Hold

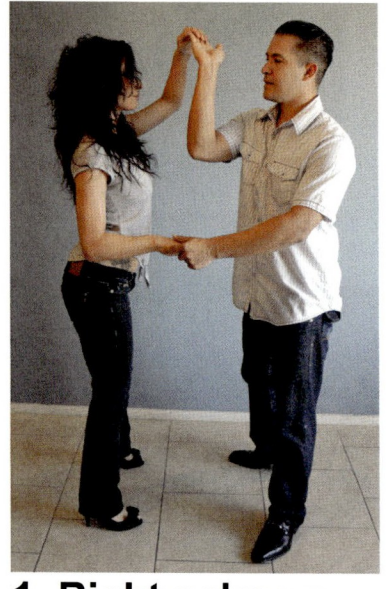

1. Right palm up

2. ½ Turn to Left

3. ½ Turn Left

4. Regain hold & Tap

5. Side Step

Beginner Tip: Guys after the second beat let go of your left hand hold between beats 2 & 3 So that you can turn & so that the ladies hand can wrap around your midsection as you turn. If you don't let go in time you'll yank her arm.

Move # 21 Mans Inside Turn-Loop & Waist Wrap

6. Together

7. Side Step

8. Tap or Hip Lift

Leader Tip: Guys notice how in photo # 1 the man has his palm facing up toward the ceiling, while keeping a finger tip hold with the lady's hand. This is a technique you'll want to practice.

There is an analogy I like to use to describe how to have your hand/arm for this move...its like a **waiters arm** when he is carrying a tray of food in his hand, his arm is upright and his palm flat facing upward. This is how you'll have your arm when you do these Bachata loops.

Mans Turn Explained:

This can be described as a <u>3 step turn</u>, just like most Bachata turns.

The first step is side with your <u>Left foot</u>.

Then do a ½ Turn to your left, Stepping on your <u>Right Foot</u>.

Do one more ½ Turn to your left, landing on your <u>Left foot</u>.

At the end of this you should be facing your partner.

Move # 22 Turn Combo & Arm Figure four Wrap

0. Two Hand Hold

1. Raise Arms & Side

2. Turn Lady

3. Mans left arm up

4. Tap Hip Lift

5. Side Step

Arms Explained: From beginning to end with this combo we keep hold of the same hands, there are no hand switches. In Photo 3 the mans <u>left arm is the higher one</u> & <u>his left is the lower one,</u> near her elbow. In Photo # 6 Release your left hand hold with the lady, leave her hand on your shoulder and keep your right hand high enough to turn under.

Move # 22 Turn Combo & Arm Figure Four Wrap

6. ½ Turn Left

7. ½ Turn left

regain 2 Hand Hold

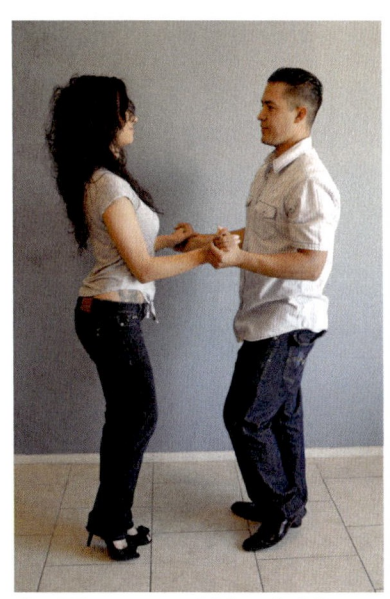

8. Tap or Hip Lift

Turn Explained: The man does an outside turn, to his left.

Step 5: Side step & prepare to turn outward on beats 6 & 7.

Step 6: Do a ½ turn to the left, landing on your left foot.

Step 7: Another ½ turn to the left, landing on your right foot, facing the lady.

Move # 23 Cross Turn & Side by Side Basic

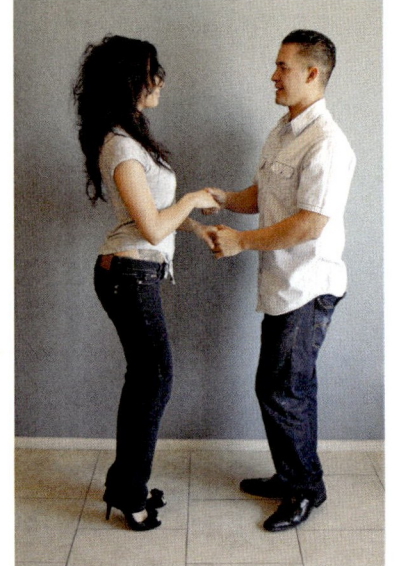
0. Right over left

1. begin Turn

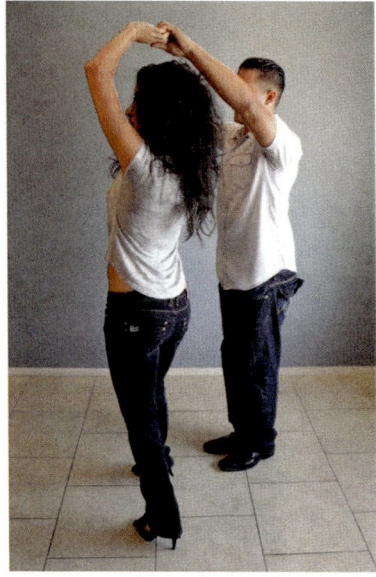
2. ½ Turn Lady

3. ½ Turn facing

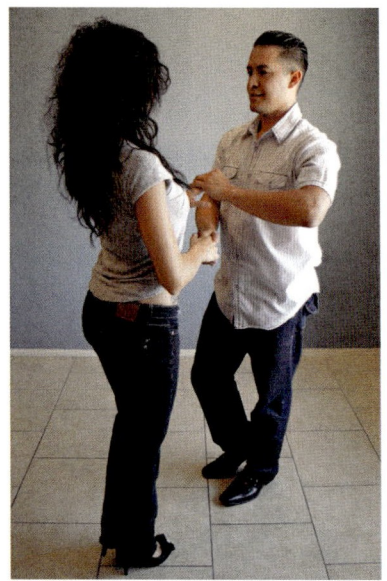
4. Tap or Hip

5. Side & Begin turn

Leaders Tip: On step 6 on the next page is when you'll lower your hands so that you get in the side by side position. Then finish the basic and begin going forward with the basic facing forward with her.

Move # 23 Cross Turn & Side By Side Basic Combo

6. ½ Turn Lady

7. ½ Turn or Less

8. Tap/ Hip Lift

1. Forward

2. Forward

3. Forward

Ladies Style Tip: You can also add a light shoulder shimmy to your forward & back basic to give you an extra rhythmical look, but the keyword is a <u>light,</u> so keep it subtle, but sexy.

Move # 23 Cross Turn & Side By Side Basic Combo...continued

4. Hip/ Tap

5. Back

6. Back

7. Back

8. Tap or Hip Lift

1. Begin Turn out

Ladies Tip: ladies have your palms facing forward, and lightly press forward with your hands so that you have a connection with your partner in this side by side position. Plus don't forget to move those hips!

Move # 23 Cross Turn Side By Side Basic Combo

2. ½ Turn Lady

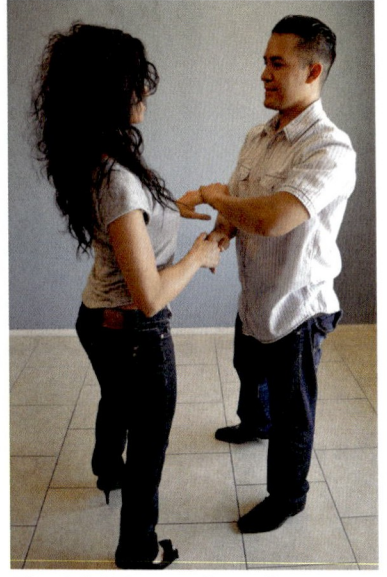

3. ½ Turn Lady

4. Tap or Hip Lift

5. Raise arms

6. together

7. Neck Loop

Beginner Tip: On Steps 5- 8 on this page, take your the 2-3 beats to do the Neck loop, you don't want to rush the neck loops, it takes away all the sexiness if you do. Rushing it would be trying to do the loop in 1 beat.

Move # 23 Cross Turn & Side by Side Basic Continued...

8. Fully Wrapped

Transition to Frame

Once you've finished the move then transition to the closed dance frame so you can move on to the next move.

The Forward & back basic is a fun and popular move in Bachata, one way to add more to the step is by **raising up your leg** or as some people call it bicycle the leg. This is supposed to be similar to the circular reverse leg action you use when you back pedal on a bicycle.

To the right is a photo example of the leg raised, with the lady's instep of her foot next to the side of her knee. With her toes pointed downward.

On the next page we'll show the Side by Side forward & back basic with this leg styling added in.

Move # 24 Forward & Back Basic with Leg Raise

0. Side Position

1. Step Forward

2. Forward

3. Forward

4. Raise *Inside leg

5. Back

Inside Leg: is the one leg closest to your partner, this is the one you raise. So the lady raises her left leg & the man raises his Right leg. If your raising the leg farthest from your partner, your doing something wrong.

Move # 24 Forward & Back Basic with Leg Raise

6. Back

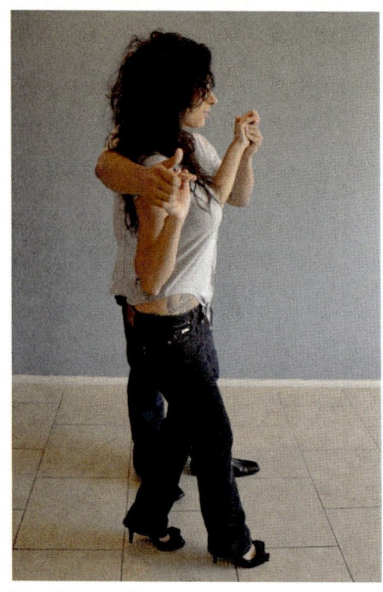
7. Back

8. Tap or Hip Lift

The "leg raise" is done on the 4th beat where you would normally tap, raise your hip or some other action to mark the beat. So you do this instead of the hip raise or foot/heel tap.

Ladies Tip: Keep both palms facing forward when your in this side by side hold, your hands should lightly press forward into the mans finger tips so that you two have a "connection".

Beginner Tip: Don't look down at your feet when you dance this move, you either want to look ahead, keeping your head up, or for a more intimate and romantic feel you can gaze at your partner.

- For detail on how to get into & out of the "Side by Side" position see move # 23 on the previous pages.

Move # 25 Cradle Walk & Neck Wrap Combo

0. Two hand Hold

1. Side

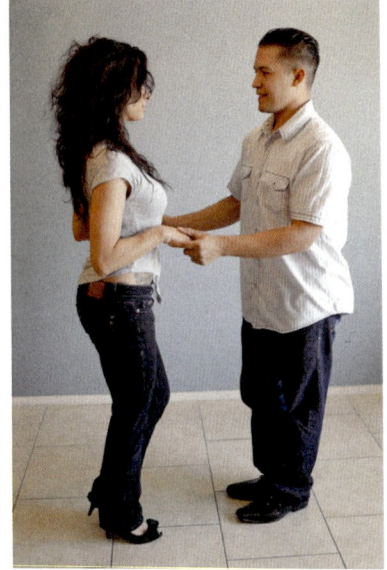
2. Together

3. Side

4. Tap or Hip Lift

5. Prep Inside turn

Lead Tip: In Photo # 5 notice how the man flips his hand so that his thumb is downward and his palm facing the girl. This is the hand position that will make the inside turn part of the Cradle easier.

Move # 25 Cradle Walk & Neck Wrap Combo, continued...

6. Wrap her in

7. Finish Turn

7. Side/back step

8. Hip or Tap

1. Forward

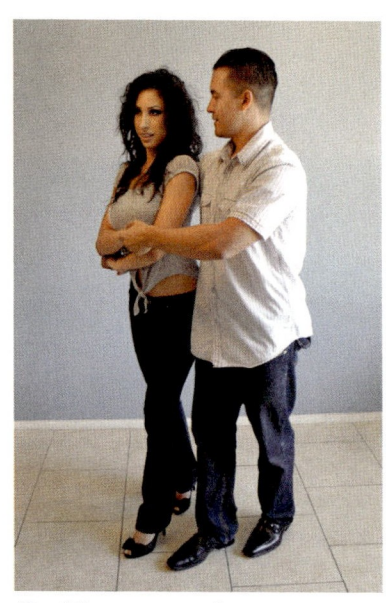

2. Forward

Beginner Tip: For a more intimate feel you can also face your partner on the walk forward. Just don't look down. Also guys be sure that you **don't squish or squeeze her arms** too tight when you have her in the cradle.

Move # 25 Cradle Walk & Neck Wrap Combo...Continued

3. Forward

4. Hip or Tap

5. Back

6. Back

7. Back

8. Tap or Hip

Style Tip: On count 4 on this page you can also do the "Leg Raise" instead of the tap or hip raise just like in move # 26. Be sure that it is the "Inside Leg" that raises up on this move.

Move # 25 Cradle Walk & Neck Wrap Combo...Continued

1. Raise arm & step

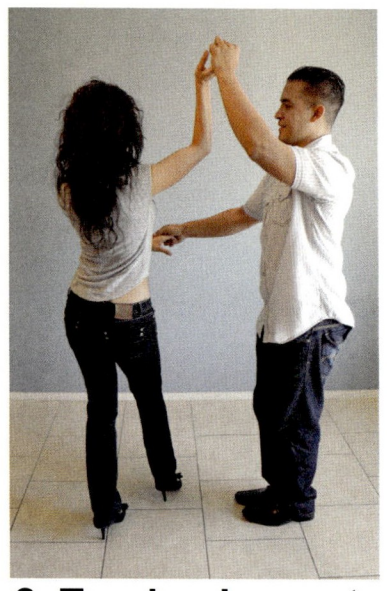

2. Turning her out

3. Side Step

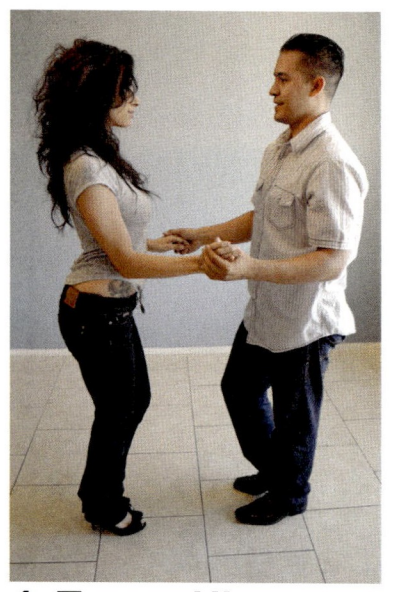

4. Tap or Hip

5. Raise right palm

6. Look Thru loop

Hip Technique: On the "Forward & Back basics" like in the Cradle walk you can still do the hip raises.

Move # 25 Cradle Walk & Neck Wrap Combo...Continued

7. Neck Loop   **8. Hold loop & tap**   **Go to Dance Frame**

For more details on how to do the mans 1 arm loop see page 36 where it is covered in more detail.

Style Tip: You can also stay in this move and dance a basic with the loop hold as a second option instead of jumping into the dance frame.

Bachata Hip Raise Demonstrated

1. Left Side, not raised   **2. Left Hip Raised**

1. Right side, not raised   **2. Right Hip Raised**

On photos #1 in both above notice that the lady has her hip out to the side, the it's raised on # 2. This is like a wind up to the hip raise. It gives the actual hip raise more effect. When you do the hip raise, press your foot into the ground to begin the hip lift, also keep your body upright. A common beginner mistake is to bend you body at the middle giving yourself a unusual shape

Ladies Bachata Upward Arm Styling

0. left Arm up

1. Behind Neck

2. Side of Head

3. Lower downward

4. To hip

This type of arm styling can be done when the man has you in a One arm hold which commonly happens after turns and other tricks. When you arm is free, add style and flavor to the way you dance with this arm move.

Ladies Arm Styling to Side

0. Neutral

1. Arm out to Side

2. Raising Arm up

3. Behind Head

4. Down side

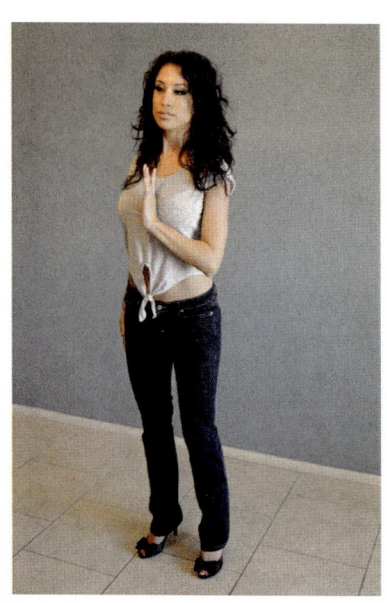

5. Past Chest

Arm styling should be practiced in front of a mirror and try to get all the positions that are shown here. The arm should flow from one position to the next.

Ladies Arm Styling to the Side...Continued

6. Return to Hip

Arm Styling can be and should be done when ever you have a free arm. The last thing you want is to just have your arm drooping at your side its not very sexy looking. So train yourself that when an arm frees up make your arm dance as well.

Your free to do this until you see the man reaching for your hand again, then you obviously need to give it to him. Because he's the leader in the dance and your the follower. So you have to go along with his lead.

Beginner Tip: Don't reach out and try to grab the man into frame & don't grab at his hands, wait for him to invite back into a hold. When he lets go of your hand think of it as an opportunity to show off your sexiness with some arm styling.

Sexy Bachata Dips

Section # 6

Move #26 Around the World Dip (Beginner Level)

0. Hands on Back

1. Rotate to Right

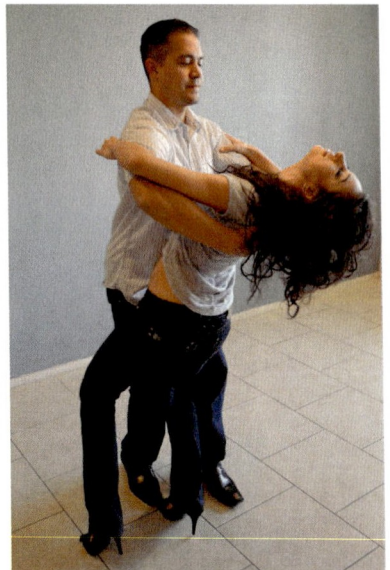
2. Head tilt Back

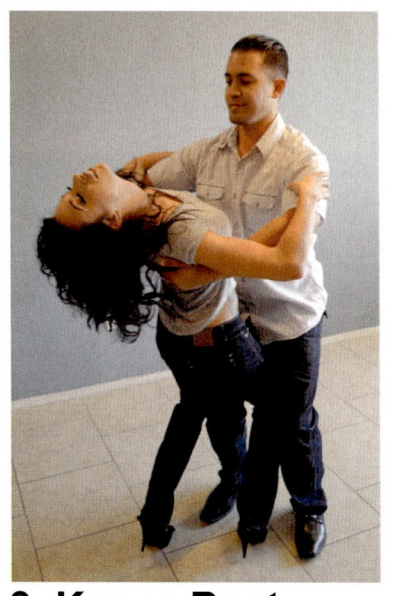
3. Knees Bent

4. Rotate her to left

5. Raise up

Ladies: Ladies must bend their knees, press their hips upward toward your partner & roll to the front of your feet to help your arch back.

Guys: Guys stay upright to counter balance her, bend knees, hips to hers.